OWNING THE
WORLD OF IDEAS

SAGE SWIFTS

In 1976 SAGE published a series of short 'university papers', which led to the publication of the QASS series (or the 'little green books' as they became known to researchers). Almost 40 years since the release of the first 'little green book', SAGE is delighted to offer a new series of swift, short and topical pieces in the ever-growing digital environment.

SAGE *Swifts* offer authors a new channel for academic research with the freedom to deliver work outside the conventional length of journal articles. The series aims to give authors speedy access to academic audiences through digital first publication, space to explore ideas thoroughly, yet at a length which can be readily digested, and the quality stamp and reassurance of peer-review.

OWNING THE
WORLD OF IDEAS
INTELLECTUAL PROPERTY AND GLOBAL
NETWORK CAPITALISM

MATTHEW DAVID
DEBORA HALBERT

Los Angeles | London | New Delhi
Singapore | Washington DC

Los Angeles | London | New Delhi
Singapore | Washington DC

SAGE Publications Ltd
1 Oliver's Yard
55 City Road
London EC1Y 1SP

SAGE Publications Inc.
2455 Teller Road
Thousand Oaks, California 91320

SAGE Publications India Pvt Ltd
B 1/I 1 Mohan Cooperative Industrial Area
Mathura Road
New Delhi 110 044

SAGE Publications Asia-Pacific Pte Ltd
3 Church Street
#10-04 Samsung Hub
Singapore 049483

© Matthew David and Debora Halbert 2015

First published 2015

Library of Congress Control Number: 2015939816

British Library Cataloguing in Publication data

A catalogue record for this book is available from
the British Library

Editor: Chris Rojek
Assistant editor: Gemma Shields
Production editor: Vanessa Harwood
Marketing manager: Michael Ainsley
Cover design: Jen Crisp
Typeset by: C&M Digitals (P) Ltd, Chennai, India
Printed and bound by CPI Group (UK) Ltd,
Croydon, CR0 4YY

ISBN 978-1-4739-1576-3
eISBN 978-1-4739-2756-8

To Johanna K. Schenner for her insights

Also

*To Daylenn Moke Alani Ka'ai Pua
and his Ohana*

David and Halbert provide a timely, concise and cosmopolitan guide to the contradictions and paradoxes that vex the systems of intellectual property that govern the so-called knowledge economy in an era of globalized informational capital. With its crisp prose and comprehensive coverage, it will be a welcome user-friendly manual to introduce students to intellectual property issues across the academy.

Rosemary J. Coombe, Canada Research Chair in Law, Communication and Culture, York University

Intellectual property is arguably the branch of law that speaks most directly to the state of capitalist society as a whole, yet until now there hasn't really been a book that makes both the field's traditional issues and cutting edge developments accessible to non-specialists in the social sciences. David and Halbert have written just such a book. *Owning the World of Ideas* is organized around the idea that intellectual property is the pivotal site for studying the interplay of regulation and de-regulation in the shaping of capitalism. The result is a stunning achievement of both comprehensiveness and concision that will be difficult to match in the future.

Steve Fuller, Auguste Comte Professor of Social Epistemology, University of Warwick, Author of *The New Sociological Imagination* and *The Sociology of Intellectual Life*

Intellectual property used to be a field for technicians, isolated in law practice and ignored by most social justice advocates. It is no longer and for good reason. Through their sustained evaluation of the concept critical in intellectual property law that ideas are a public good and unownable as private property, Halbert and David demonstrate how preserving the freedom of ideas in the face of global economic inequality and the inevitability of digital connectivity in the 21st century is critical to democratic engagement, health and human flourishing.

Jessica Sibley, Professor of Law, Suffolk University Law School

In *Owning the World of Ideas*, David and Halbert offer an incisive, critical and powerful analysis of information capitalism, focusing on its monopolisation of knowledge and culture through increasingly aggressive structures of intellectual ownership. The authors present a timely counter to these trends, arguing instead for an approach to intellectual property that favours human well-being over and above the economic expropriation and monopolisation of knowledge. This is an important book which deserves a wide and appreciative audience.

Majid Yar, Professor of Sociology and Associate Director: Centre for Criminology & Criminal Justice (CCCJ), University of Hull

Owning the World of Ideas is a stimulating situation report on current political and legal struggles over intellectual property (IP), regarded only a few decades ago as the exclusive domain of specialist lawyers and economists. Written for a general readership by two well-known IP scholars, this well-researched book shows that while *juridical IP control through copyright, patents, trademarks and other mechanisms is constantly expanding into* new areas, IP rights are often ignored by the broad public and are frequently technically unenforceable. The authors describe how these various IP systems work, their defects, who benefits from them, the harm that they often cause, and forms that resistance has taken. By debunking overreaching claims that IP incentivises creativity, facilitates the spread of innovation and supports quality control, this accessible book will help to counterbalance often aggressive pro-IP propaganda from industry organisations.

Dr Colin Darch, Democratic Governance and Rights Unit, Faculty of Law, University of Cape Town

CONTENTS

ABOUT THE AUTHORS

Matthew David teaches sociology at Durham University (UK). He is the author of *Peer to Peer and the Music Industry: The Criminalization of Sharing* (Theory, Culture and Society Monograph Series 2010), *Social Research: An Introduction* (second edition, with Carole D. Sutton, Sage 2011), *Science in Society* (Palgrave 2005) and *Knowledge Lost in Information* (with David Zeitlyn and Jane Bex, Office of Humanities Press 1998). He recently completed editing (with Debora Halbert, Sage 2014) *The Sage Handbook of Intellectual Property* and (with Peter Millward, Sage 2014) the four-volume *Researching Society Online*. His research on file-sharing, live-streaming and new media has been published in *British Journal of Sociology; European Journal of Social Theory; Sport in Society; Perspectives on Global Development and Technology;* and *Crime, Media, Culture;* as well as in the *Oxford Handbook of Internet Studies* (edited by William H. Dutton 2013). Research on other aspects of science and technology in society has been published in *Sociological Research Online; New Genetics and Society; Current Sociology; International Sociology; Telematics and Informatics; Systemica;* and *Sociology Compass.* He is interested in the potential for sharing in an age beyond scarcity and is currently writing a book to be called *Sharing: Crime against Capitalism?*

Debora Halbert is Professor of Political Science at the University of Hawaii at Manoa where she teaches futures studies, public policy and courses in law and society. In addition to being Chair for the Political Science Department, Halbert is a faculty affiliate with the Hawaii Research Center for Futures Studies. The bulk of her academic publications deal with intellectual property in the digital world, with an even more targeted focus on copyright law. Her most recent book, *The State of Copyright: The Complex Relationships of Culture Creation in a Globalized World,* was published by Routledge in 2014. Her previous books include *Intellectual Property in the Information Age: The Politics of Expanding Ownership Rights* (Quorum 1999) and *Resisting Intellectual Property* (Routledge 2005). She has also published numerous articles on intellectual property as it relates to politics, culture, technology and the law. Her work on intellectual property is situated more broadly within a concern and interest in digital politics, the impact of information technology and the future impacts of technology on social structures including politics, law and education. Thus, issues of file-sharing, privacy, digital politics, digital democracy, technology futures and the concept of neuropolitics define additional research interests. Halbert was recently a visiting scholar with Lund University's Pufendorf Institute working with members of the Lund Internet Institute on privacy, security and internet issues. She continues to collaborate with LUii on these issues.

PREFACE

CAN THEY/CAN'T THEY? DO THEY/DON'T THEY? SHOULD THEY/SHOULDN'T THEY?

The title of this book presents a stark possibility. Some would say it is not possible. *Ownership* suggests the most forceful conception of control. *World* invokes everything there is. Given the intellectual property (IP) implications of the Outer Space Treaty, we could have said *Universe*. *Ideas* cover that which most defines what it means to be human, both as individual minds and as an inter-subjective species. Owning the world of ideas is then a tall order. Might our title then be mere hyperbole? Formally, ownership of ideas is legally impossible and, at a global level, can never be fully achieved. Yet, in very real and significant ways, these limits have been undone.

Can they/Can't they? Firstly, in every domain of IP a distinction is drawn between abstractions and their tangible manifestations. In all cases, in all jurisdictions, in principle, the manifestation can be owned while the abstraction/ knowledge being expressed cannot. As such, in principle, ideas simply cannot be *owned*. While the principle remains, undoing the distinction underpinning the principle allows its force to be undone and its meaning hollowed out. In the domain of copyright, the distinction between idea and expression has been radically diminished in recent years such that grounds for infringement claims have widened as the space of common culture and fair use has diminished. Similarly, in patent law, the distinction between invention and discovery, novel object and new knowledge of pre-existing things, has been eroded. Likewise, around trademark and related domains the scope for ownership is widened as the distinction between specific symbol and wider culture is reduced.

Do they/Don't they? If it is then possible to own ideas, how far has this actually gone in the world? To the extent that ownership has been extended further across the world of ideas, it is not absolute, nor is it fully secure. Nevertheless, in many respects this extension is very real. The post-Cold War global network capitalist world is premised upon regulatory structures – in particular the World Trade Organization, which seeks to enforce *deregulation* in global markets and production; and its Trade Related Aspects of Intellectual Property (TRIPS) Treaty, which seeks to enforce global *regulation* of IP. TRIPS and the World Intellectual Property Organization have rolled out IP extension and harmonization – in duration, geographical scope and depth of coverage – which at one level does amount to global ownership of the world of ideas. Yet, this roll-out has not been without resistance and limitations. In some cases opposition has been successful – whether in the form of legislative blockage or through new forms of informal infringement practices.

Post-Cold War neo-liberal globalization – global regulation to protect property holders, and in particular IP monopolies, combined with a deregulation of securities for everyone else – has not had everything its own way, but nonetheless remains the dominant economic and political order – for now. However, global network capitalism in its neo-liberal form is riddled with internal contradictions. Globalization, the affordances of digital networks and even the contradiction within capitalism itself between private (intellectual) property and 'pirate' free-marketeers mean that with even the best will (brute force, law, encryption and surveillance) in the world, IP monopolies cannot fully control even that which they now claim to own. If possession is nine-tenths of the law, file-sharing, generic medicines and counterfeit fashion show that formal ownership over the world of ideas, while real, is far from secure.

Should they/Shouldn't they? Given the scope and limits of owning the world of ideas, in both principle and practice, how 'should' we respond? In this book we debunk the three key justifications given for intellectual property rights (IPRs): (a) that IP incentivizes more than it inhibits creativity and innovation; (b) that IP is the best means for facilitating the distribution of new creations and innovations; and (c) that IPRs are the best means of maintaining quality and standards for both consumers and primary producers. In so doing we dismiss the arguments put forward for global extension and harmonization of IP and suggest that roll-back, suspension and, in some cases, simply the bypassing of IP offer better solutions for promoting innovation and meeting human needs.

Matthew David and Debora J. Halbert
Manoa, Hawaii
March 2015

ACKNOWLEDGEMENTS

We would like to gratefully acknowledge the intellectual contributions made by the many contributors to *The Sage Handbook of Intellectual Property*, which inspired this work. Their scholarship defines the newest thinking in the field, and editing a volume of their contributions made it possible to write this book. These include Ann Barron, Sarah Louisa Phythian-Adams, Shubha Ghosh, Daniel Gervais, Peter K. Yu, Salvador Millaleo, Hugo Cadenas, Alex Perullo, Andrew Eisenberg, Margaret Chon, Chris Rojek, Rosemary J. Coombe, Sarah Ives, Daniel Huizenga, Chidi Oguamanam, Colin Darch, Lillian Alvarez, Lee Edwards, Bethany Klein, David Lee, Giles Moss, Fiona Philip, Dave O'Brien, Jyh-An Lee, Pradip Ninan Thomas, Lisa Dobbin, Martin J. Zeilinger, Raizel Liebler, Claudy Op den Kamp, John Tehranian, Andrew Kirton, Peter Millward, Natasha Whiteman, Greg Lastowka, Jessica Silbey, Uma Suthersanen, Ian Brown, David Wall, Graham Dutfield, Susanna H. S. Leong, Jake Dunagan, William R. Kramer and Matthew Rimmer. We would also like to thank Gemma Shields at SAGE for her patience and advice along the way.

LIST OF ABBREVIATIONS

ACTA – Anti-Counterfeiting Trade Agreement

CDC – Centers for Disease Control and Prevention

CDR – Community Design Regulation

CJEU – Court of Justice of the European Union

FDI – foreign direct investment

GATT – General Agreement on Tariffs and Trade

GMO – genetically modified organism

GI – geographical indicator

IP – intellectual property

IPR – intellectual property rights

UPOV – International Union for the Protection of New Varieties of Plants

MICO – marks indicating conditions of origin

TPB – The Pirate Bay

TRIPS – Trade Related Aspects of Intellectual Property

TK – traditional knowledge

TKDP – Traditional Knowledge Digital Project

TTIP – Transatlantic Trade and Investment Partnership

TNC – transnational corporation

TPP – Trans-Pacific Partnership

UCC – Universal Copyright Convention

USPTO – US Patent and Trade Office

WIPO – World Intellectual Property Organization

WTO – World Trade Organization

I
KEY CONCEPTS AND WHY THEY MATTER SO MUCH TODAY

Intellectual property (IP) has a history bound up with the rise of capitalism. Intellectual property rights (IPRs) extend monopoly control over a range of immaterial things, thereby excluding competition and maintaining or increasing profits for the rights holder. In recent decades neo-liberal policies have deregulated labour markets while strengthening IPRs regulation globally. Physical production costs have fallen while value added from IP has risen. Market forces are used to discipline labour, but monopolies have developed to protect property and in particular IP. By using IPRs to halt competition, prohibitions against 'legal' market entry (illegal or pirate market entry may still be available) lead to super-profits (profits in excess of what a competitive market would afford). This situation makes IP infringement increasingly attractive and in some cases the only opportunity for economic participation.

The formation of today's global network society was not simply the liberation of culture, politics and economics from the 'dead hand' of state regulation, whether in the form of western Keynesianism or in the form of the former Soviet Union and its satellites. The post-Cold War construction of today's global world has involved a very particular combination of regulation and deregulation and is not a 'natural' consequence of the end of history or the triumph of the free-market. The establishment of the World Trade Organization (WTO) and its first act, the creation of the Agreement on Trade Related Aspects of Intellectual Property (TRIPS), set up a very particular ratchet that has been neo-liberal globalization's governing principle ever since – on the one hand, the increased global regulation of IPRs and, on the other, the further global deregulation of labour.

This book seeks to trace this ratchet through the myriad types of IP, the construction of the concept of IP itself and how the global ownership of IP may shape our future lives. We will investigate the role of global IPRs in staking out ownership over the world of ideas. The rise of the global network society, a concept developed by Manuel Castells, has been accompanied by an equal rise in the significance of IPRs as a core set of regulatory principles governing human interaction and inequality in a world where information flows through and beyond traditional boundaries and formal borders. Yet, it would be a mistake to believe that the rise of a network society, where technology makes possible both global connectedness and large-scale automation of what was once the greater part of human labour, inevitably led to the greater economic valuation of 'ideas' relative to 'physical labour'. This has been a path chosen, and yet one that has been challenged and which is not set in stone. In this chapter we lay out the basics of IP, what the concept entails and how the paradoxes of a capitalist IP system shape the global flow of ideas.

GLOBAL NETWORK CAPITALISM AND THE TRIPLE PARADOX OF IP

In today's global network capitalism, IP has become more fundamental than ever for three reasons – the enhanced globalization, digitalization and capitalization of the world – themselves the three key elements in today's global network capitalism. However, each of these elements is contradictory to the point of being paradoxical – at least in terms of the significance of IP. Through all three of these processes, IP is becoming more significant than ever, yet in all three dimensions IP is more seriously hard to control, and is therefore more vulnerable, than it has ever been before.

The Paradox of Globalization for IP: The Transnational Firm, Outsourcing and Global Supply Networks

The neo-liberal form of today's global network capitalism promotes what Robert Frank and Philip Cook (1996) call a 'winner takes all' economy. *Regulation* to protect property is combined with *deregulation* to increase competition between workers. The roll-out of global property protection is particularly focused upon enforcement of IPRs beyond borders. This has fuelled the growth of global IP monopoly holding firms (the world bestriding transnational corporations – TNCs). These companies have ruthlessly outsourced manufacturing across the planet to reduce labour and regulation costs. While production is moved elsewhere to be done by others, TNCs still claim the right to own the finished product and, in the case of IP-protected goods, the right to be the only ones allowed to sell such products. As such, global deregulation of production and regulation of IP offers TNCs the best of both worlds, minimizing costs while at the same time maximizing profits by retaining control and excluding competition. A handbag designed in London, for example, can now be manufactured in and shipped from China at a labour cost only a tiny fraction of the price the trademark-branded object can then command back in London (or even in China itself). The same cost reduction and global distribution works for medicine, auto parts, cigarettes and clothing.

Nonetheless, the creation of global trade and production networks challenges the ability of IP-rich TNCs to fully control that which they claim to own. Outsourcing might reduce cost and legal liability, but it also makes it harder to control the release of unauthorized extra copies being made and circulated outside the control of the commissioning corporation. Reduced border controls on manufactured goods and the containerization of transportation also increase the scope for such *overproduction* to circulate as widely as *authorized* products. Foreign direct and indirect investment linked to reducing costs and/or outsourcing production also lead to the transfer of IP-rich technology that is then reverse-engineered and reproduced illicitly around the world. Global flows of technical labour also transfer valuable knowledge beyond IP control.

While IP evasion is most evident in the copyright field, where file-sharing software allows digital copies of content to be freely circulated more efficiently than either IP holders or commercial pirates can match (see next section), global supply networks enable making and purchase of generic drugs, counterfeit branded goods and even seeds, beyond corporate IP holder control.

Thus, IP's first paradox is that while global trade and production capabilities extend the scope of TNCs to reduce costs and expand markets in ideas, at the same time global supply networks afford alternative global connections that evade IP controls.

The Paradox of Digital Networks for IP: Networks of Control Versus the Empowered Network Individual

What Manuel Castells (2000a) calls the rise of the network society combines a technical mode of development with a continued capitalist mode of production. Cold War arms spending, state welfare expansion, automated manufacturing and international corporate trade expansion (noted above) all fuelled the rise of network computing, but digital networks have themselves come to drive forward change in new directions. As Castells (2009, 86) notes, the creation of a global digital network media architecture, the collapse of the Soviet Union (and the subsequent roll-out of a totalizing capitalist globalization), as well as a new global framework for trade and IP (the WTO and its first-born TRIPS), all came together in the formation of today's global network capitalism. International trade, itself a prior driver of network development, is also boosted today by the ability not just to coordinate trade globally but to distribute production via digital networks. Digital production, coordination and distribution reduce costs and expand markets. The reduction of costs is at its most extreme in the realm of pure digital goods (software, music, film, television, etc.), but the same market networks for digital goods also intensify the control revolution in the production and distribution of patented, trademarked and other IP-protected goods.

The scale of cost reduction and market expansion afforded by the new digital networks is staggering, but it has an Achilles' heel for the globalized economic system. Just as the perfect profit storm afforded by global digital networks first hit the music industry in the 1980s with the advent of the CD, so it was the music industry that first felt the full force of free digital online file-sharing in the late 1990s (David 2010, 2013). The challenge to IP posed by small-scale actors right down to the level of networked individual consumers has been enhanced and globalized. The rising threat of individual consumers has led to a shift in law towards the prosecution of individuals for IP infringement. Such individualization is a radical departure. In the past the threat of infringement came from commercial actors capable of making the physical objects required to use IP content, not the fans, consumers and end-users of that content. Today's IP infringement has been disintermediated. For example, a computer user can copy any amount of copyright-rich content without the need to press records or manufacture video cassettes, etc. The development of 3D printers (see Rifkin 2014) means that the same globalization of individual agency will soon enable internet users to start downloading trademark fashions, patented drugs and industrial design objects just as they already download or stream music, film television and software.

The network mode of development is not reducible to network capitalism. Legal monopolies have been redrafted and bolstered. However, their technical circumvention continues to outmanoeuvre all such attempts to clamp down. What started in music now encompasses the whole cultural sector and beyond. The second paradox of IP is that while digital content is formally protected for sale worldwide, digitization also makes content freely available to everyone everywhere.

The Paradox of Capitalism for IP: Property Versus Markets

The most counterintuitive paradox of IP within today's global network capitalism is one within the supposed essential character of capitalism itself, its synthesis of private property and free-markets. It may be assumed that property rights and free-markets are essentially compatible bedfellows within capitalism. If one person is to sell another person a loaf of bread, it must be assumed it is the first person's to sell, and that the second had no right to take it without paying.

Property is a necessary condition for market exchange. However, IPRs extend a conception of property (one that will be examined in more detail as this book progresses) beyond any particular object to the right to make copies of that object (and in the case of IPRs – intangible object). This creates monopolies in the provision of those objects protected, prohibiting competition (market entry) and hence enabling higher prices. The extension of property rights over the copying of intangible goods is therefore antithetical to the existence of free-markets, and limits have almost always been placed upon IPRs accordingly. However, in recent years, such limits have been reduced, increasing the significance of the paradox of capitalism in relation to IPRs – strong IP suspends markets in the interests of protecting property.

Colin Crouch (2011, 7) notes the distinction between 'ordo-liberalism' (anti-trust regulation of mergers to prevent competition leading to the suspension of markets such as when dominant players buy up smaller ones and hence create monopoly conditions) and 'neo-liberalism' (which defends private property even to the extent that unregulated competition allows dominant competitors to buy up and/or drive out weaker rivals and hence suspend real market conditions). Ordo-liberalism requires authorities to break up monopolies to preserve free-markets (such as when the US National Football League introduced the 'draft' system to ensure that successful teams in earlier seasons did not monopolize all the good players in the following seasons – perpetuating success but reducing the excitement of the competition). In contrast 'neo-liberalism' promotes – and has been promoted by – the growth of powerful TNCs. Neo-liberal policies have allowed for the elimination of competition by TNCs, promoting their monopoly position with powerful extensions of IP to reduce competition further and, as such, prioritizing property over markets for powerful actors even as deregulated labour markets are used to further discipline non-property owners.

Today's global network capitalism has adopted the neo-liberal pathway. However, there is a catch. IP protection promotes 'pirate' markets and anti-capitalist sharing. IP monopolies inflate prices and so encourage a pirate capitalism which functions as a shadow-market providing consumers with access to IP-protected products at more affordable prices. IPRs also encourage forms of 'anti-capitalist' sharing, which infringes IPRs not for profit but simply to access use-values without their sublimation under exchange-value. Thus, the third paradox is that while IP is necessary to maintain scarcity and hence a 'market' at least in the sense of ideas being sold at all, IP monopolies suspend the free-market itself to defend property rights, but in so doing encourage piracy and sharing alternatives.

THE SIGNIFICANCE OF IP IN A GLOBAL NETWORK WORLD

Global tensions regarding the protection, sharing and use of those things covered by IP laws abound. Take, for example, recent concerns over patenting genes. While not the first of its kind, Myriad Genetics' 1994 and 1995 patents on genes linked to breast cancer were a global legal victory that exemplified the extension of IP from protecting inventions of novel, useful and new things to also protecting the 'discovery' of natural and already existing processes. While the patents were issued in 1994/5, a 2013 US Supreme Court decision revoked Myriad's BRCA gene patents (but not the cDNA patents), thus marking a momentary retreat from the extension of IP ownership over the 'natural' world (Barraclough 2013). However, even as Myriad lost its battle to own the BRCA gene, multiple other living organisms and genetic sequences remain patented and thus controlled via IP laws (Leong 2014).

A second example concerns copyright. The 1998 US Digital Millennium Copyright Act, which signed into domestic US law the conditions of the WTO's TRIPS treaty, criminalized the creation and use of any technology that could be used to violate copyright. This anti-circumvention legislation targets those technologies that have the capacity to unlock the digital rights management associated with control of music, open e-books so that blind readers can have access to the text and offer methods for users to more freely use their devices. While the full impact of anti-circumvention laws has been tempered by 'dual use', 'fair use' and/or 'fair dealing' rulings which create 'safe harbours' and space for expression, again, IP lobbyists are pressing hard to extend, widen and deepen protections and further contain what they claim to be unauthorized use of culture.

Globally, not all countries have adopted the same attitude towards IP protection. Brazil's 2014 legalization of 'generic' medicines challenges the global expansion of transnational pharmaceutical companies' IP claims. In the face of resistance, treaties like the highly secretive Transatlantic Trade and Investment Partnership (TTIP) between the US and EU, and Trans-Pacific Partnership (TPP) between the US and East Asia seek to bind states into upholding the IPRs of transnational firms, rights that cover a diversity of products from medicines, seeds, designer goods, music, books, computer programs and much more. Such transnational treaties, negotiated in secret with the interests of industry in clear sight, are designed to bypass resistance to the expansion of IP, even if not always successfully. Resistance to IP efforts to establish monopoly controls via transnational agreements remain globally significant. These resistances in the name of citizen rights and access to such things as affordable health care, education; the right to participate in cultural life and to freedom of expression present a different global approach to development concerns.

These tensions are at the heart of a world in which information as property has become central to the global political economy. The global flow of goods – accompanied by the abstraction of property rights so that IP coverage is increasingly extended as the distinctions between 'ideas', 'tangible expressions' and 'physical carriers' is diminished, and even more importantly the right to reproduce, innovate upon or copy these objects – makes essential a global debate over the scope and limitation of IPRs in a free society and culture.

WHAT ARE IPR'S?

IP is a social contract, a legal protection extended by society to the holder(s) of such rights. This protection affords the holder certain privileges when it comes to using and/or selling access to use. IP protection, therefore, constitutes a limitation on use by others such that the IPR holder has some degree of monopoly control over that to which the rights pertain. The duration of such monopoly controls varied greatly historically and between different forms of IP. The extent of control has also varied between states. Recent attempts to 'harmonize' such differences between national IP regimes have highlighted the significance of IP today as well as the significance of the drivers that have pushed for such a global regime (Halbert 1999; May 2000; Sell 2003; Richards 2004; Gervais 2007, 2014).

All rights and laws are social contracts. Ideas of natural justice and claims to 'find' universal rights that transcend the specific conventions of particular regimes, while potentially ethically valid (Held 2010), are only substantiated if enforced by social institutions (Rawls 1971). That all rights are social contracts is particularly important to recall in the case of IP, as debates about IP get confused when the question of whether IP should be seen as 'property' gets raised. It is often forgotten that physical 'property' is also just a legal (and therefore a social) convention. Contemporary debates over IP suggest that a similar erasure of the social construction of rights has occurred in this field as well.

Intellectual?

What counts as 'intellectual' in the case of IPRs? The term intellectual here is used to refer to products of the human mind. By product is meant a tangible expression of mental activity, not 'an idea' in abstraction. Copyright covers expressions, not pure ideas; patents cover manifestations of invention shown to be useful, original and non-obvious, not speculative inventions that cannot be seen to 'work'; trademarks cover recognizable signs, not general symbols, etc. However, the distinctions between an idea and its expression, as between an invention and a discovery, or between a specific sign and a generic symbol, are not clear-cut and so become the substance of ongoing and significant dispute in courts, legislatures and in academic commentary. In addition to its increasing economic significance, temporal extension and geographical spread, attempts to widen and deepen the intellectual 'reach' of IPRs (what gets covered) can be seen as a move towards what we have termed 'owning the world of ideas'.

The distinctions between general idea/specific expression, discovery/invention, specific/generic signs, etc., are not themselves self-evident. Thus, decisions have to be made to balance the danger of offering monopoly control over too much of general culture or the natural world against the opposite danger of offering too little incentive to those that would create novelty and progress in 'ideas'. Offering protection to products of the mind seeks to afford such products something of the security physical things possess by dint of firstly their sheer physical form and secondly the application of the notion of 'property' to them (and hence the protection of law). Taking an 'idea' is easier than taking a table or even a spoon, though taking an idea is not the same as removing it, as would be the case if one were to 'take' a spoon. To take an idea is to copy it, not to remove it. Also, extending property rights to non-things is problematic for the same reason it may seem necessary in the first place. If the expression of an idea, of an invention or of a recognizable sign needs protection because it can be so easily copied, there is a danger that overly protecting expressions/inventions/signs might itself choke off any future creative work/invention/trade. Future works of the mind will almost inevitably draw upon and resemble past works. Too long or too extensive a form of protection would make all future creativity an act of infringement.

Strong IP defenders seek to minimize the distinction between idea and expression, between discovery and invention and between specific identifiers and generic symbols, signs and language itself, so as to extend protection as far 'up' into 'ideas' as possible (Fuller and Lipinska 2014). Strong IP critics (Vaidhyanathan 2003; Lessig 2005) seek to maximize these distinctions even to the point of detachment (such that every 'expression' is seen as unique and hence remains totally 'free' within a shared and common culture). The scope of protection remains a constant tension underlying the global debate on IP.

Property?

Despite claims to the contrary and the general belief that one might be able to assert a property right over ideas, IP is not 'property' pure and simple. A distinction is drawn between IP and physical property. Whereas property rights over a house, a car or a spoon are generally 'absolute' and 'perpetual', IPRs are designed to be limited. Ownership in ideas, even when this is limited to creative, functional or recognizable manifestations, creates a monopoly in 'knowledge' that inhibits future creativity and thus is not the same as owning a house, a car or a spoon.

Most particularly, IPRs are, with one exception, time-limited. As such, IPRs are manifestly balanced 'social contracts' between society and creators/ inventors. Society extends 'quasi-property' protection to rights holders as a reward/incentive for their efforts. In exchange, the creator/inventor's work eventually becomes the common property of society when the protection runs out. This balancing of interests between creator and society makes IPRs more obviously 'social contracts' than is the case with physical property – where the term 'private property' emphasises owner rights over the balancing of interests (May and Sell 2006).

Time-limitedness in IPRs is then distinct from perpetual ownership in physical property. However, there are exceptions. Trademarks are perpetual so long as they remain in use, and physical property rights are not always absolute and may not always be perpetual, as various environmental, planning/zoning, squatting and adverse possession regulations attest. However, historically and in contemporary debates over IP, the question of whether IPRs should or should not be perpetual has been and is discussed in terms of whether or not IP should be understood as property 'like any other'. Yet, 'perpetual' property rights in things are also a social contract, not a natural 'property' of things (such as apples having the property of sweetness, or birds naturally having the property of flight). All legal protections are 'social' contracts. In our capitalist societies, perpetual property rights in things have come to be taken as 'natural' and hence a benchmark against which to measure the seemingly 'artificial' construction of less absolute rights (Piketty 2014). However, claiming something is a natural right does not make it so. As we will discuss in the next chapter, it is precisely in a context where claims that IPRs are 'property' rights are so readily asserted, taken for granted and assumed to thereby be natural that understanding the social nature of both IP and physical property rights is important.

Rights?

The terms 'intellectual' and 'property' stand as totemic symbols within culture and economics (Phythian-Adams 2014). Similarly, 'rights' carry a sense of absolute, universal and inalienable deserts in and by means of politics and law, just as the term 'property' stands as an absolute for some in the economic domain. Those who hold most to the idea that property ownership should be a fundamental human right find absolute claims to other rights (such as to education, shelter and asylum) an affront to property rights when taxation is levied on property holders to fund these other social rights (Hayek 1946; Friedman 2002). However, Thomas Piketty's (2014) international bestseller advocating global and progressive taxation on wealth and its reception indicates a renewed debate over the balance to be struck between property rights and other social rights.

The demand that IPRs should be upheld in countries other than that of the rights holder parallels claims that citizens (or stateless persons) should have their rights upheld in, and even by, regimes other than their own (Held 2010). This extension is termed 'national treatment'. However, when rights appear to clash as they sometimes do between the variety of property and social rights, how might they be balanced? Are some rights inalienable, while others can and should be traded/set aside (see Brown 2014)? Advocates of strong IPRs argue that IPRs, like physical property rights, should be understood as 'universal human rights' alongside universal rights such as those to shelter, food, education and free expression (Helfer and Austin 2011). If so, all member states of the UN would have an obligation to uphold foreign and domestic IPRs just as they are required to shelter refugees, feed the starving and educate children. IP critics argue that IPRs are lesser rights than those that warrant access to food, medicine and education, and, as such, IPRs may reasonably be limited/suspended if in doing so greater fulfilment of 'higher' material rights (such as when medical patents are suspended in order to supply affordable health care – Halbert 2005, 87–111) and non-material rights (such as in accessing educational and cultural resources – Álvarez 2014) is achieved.

Just as the terms 'intellectual' and 'property' fail to give the term 'intellectual property rights' absolute fixity, neither does the term 'rights'. Rights may or may not be extended to cover certain groups for certain entitlements, and rights may or may not be traded, overridden or treated as 'universal'. What has unfolded over time and what currently stands is a balance of competing claims and counterclaims made by shifting alliances of social actors. As such, just as IPRs are central to maintaining and intensifying contemporary global network capitalism, so it is power and resistance within global network society that is key to shaping the present and future of IPRs (Halbert 2005; David 2010).

Who?

Protecting IPRs is not always the same as protecting the artist/inventor who produced the work. IPRs can be 'alienated'. Authors and musicians sell copyrights to publishers and record labels in exchange for royalties. Employers can claim ownership over the innovations of their staff. Universities can sell their IPRs to private companies. Over time there has been a consolidation of IPRs into corporate hands (Halbert 2014).

Generally speaking, IPRs are held by individuals who create something new, though the bar for creativity in copyright is set quite low. The copyright owner, however, controls the reproduction of a copyrighted work and also controls many possible transformative uses of their work. So, for example, if a new work of art is 'substantially similar' to an already existing work, it may be deemed a copyright infringement by the courts. This was the case in the US court decision in *Rogers v. Koons* (1992), where Jeff Koons produced a sculpture based upon a postcard he found entitled 'A String of Puppies'. Despite the fact Koons argued his work was transformative, in part because it was a sculpture and not a photograph, and in part because it was a parody of American banality, the court found that he had infringed the copyright of the photographer.

Patents also are designed to protect that which is novel. However, patents especially those written broadly may cover a substantial range of possible future products. In patent law, the demand for novelty in inventions should prevent possible claims of ownership over aspects of the common culture and prior art. Patent law specifically prohibits patents on those inventions seen as part of prior art. However, while in theory the public domain should be protected, in practice there have been numerous cases where indigenous and traditional community practices have been prey to 'biopiracy/bioprospecting' and other forms of cultural appropriation. Indigenous knowledge in the 'public domain' where existing group knowledge is simply copied by outsiders with no reward or recognition being 'paid' to the originators/custodians of that knowledge is one of the political dilemmas created by a capitalist system of IPRs (Shiva 1997).

Recent additions to the stable of IPRs include rights over geographical indications (GIs) and other possible mechanisms for protecting traditional knowledge (TK). Such rights are in effect assigned to reward custodians for prior innovations and, as such, differ markedly from the logic/rationale given for IPRs in general, which is to reward innovation rather than to reward preservation. That trademarks can be issued in perpetuity also incentivizes preservation over innovation.

Moves to further extend both copyright and patent terms mean the holder of IPRs is increasingly the preserver of old knowledge rather than the creator of new knowledge. Minimizing the distinction between expression and idea, and making claims far more generic, will also give today's copyright holder far greater scope to claim future expressions that impinge their rights. The same will be true if invention is allowed to further extend into what was once deemed discovery, as even the basic building blocks of reality will become subject to patent thickets (laying down speculative patent claims on basic knowledge so that future developments which have to 'pass through' the thicket find themselves having to pay substantial 'rent').

Why?

Laws and rights are social contracts supposedly protecting members of society, however defined. Such a contract may be said to reflect natural or divine order, a bulwark against a state of nature that would otherwise be 'nasty, brutish and short' (Hobbes 2008), or a distortion of natural harmony in the interests of powerful actors (Rousseau 2008). The Hobbesian vision of an absolute monarch issuing arbitrary rights, patents and monopolies to favoured subjects and others to further the strategic interest of the state describes rather well the world prior to the legal formalization of IPRs – which started in the 18th century.

Regarding the legal formalization of such IPRs, popular rationales refer back to Locke (1988) and/or Hegel (1991). For Locke, rights over property extend from the investment of labour. Property rights are seen as 'natural justice' based upon the effort undertaken to establish physical and, by extension, mental properties. For Hegel, less in contrast than in (historical but not natural) extension of Locke, ownership rights in ideas should be accorded as a moral extension of the creator's personality (itself – for Hegel – a uniquely modern – but no less legitimate for that – recognized identity), a right to be recognized as the creator as indicated by the fact the work carries 'your' name.

In Locke's labour theory, tilling the soil creates a claim to that land (in colonial conditions blurring the distinction between discovery and creation – Shiva 1997). Whether developing a new plough gives rights over future uses of all such ploughs is less clearly the logical extension of Locke's view because the development of a new plough is contingent upon earlier versions. Thus, to accommodate these more social aspects of immaterial property, as noted above, some form of time limit on 'ownership' in ideas might follow, even if Locke's theory of natural justice regarding physical property is typically regarded as warranting perpetual ownership. The time limit demarcates the difference between labour spent making a particular physical object property (which remains 'rivalrous', meaning it cannot be used by others without reducing its utility to the first user) and time spent on an idea that – if successful – could be used by everyone at the same time – a 'non-rivalrous' good. A perpetual monopoly over a 'non-rivalrous' good would create a reward to its inventor so great, and hence a cost to society so high, that society might reasonably feel that granting protection over that innovation should only be for a fixed term. Otherwise, a perpetual monopoly will force everyone to keep paying monopoly rents or remain excluded from accessing the idea.

It should be noted that interpretations of Locke are divided. Some emphasize Locke's argument for 'natural justice' in property ownership based on effort expended and assert that such 'natural justice' is as true for ideas as for physical products. Such a view sees rights in IP as no less a natural and perhaps perpetual right than those over physical things. This extension of Locke is typically referred to as the 'natural rights' theory in IP. While never absolute, this view has held greater sway with British law makers than with legislators elsewhere. Where this view is most strongly held is among IP holders themselves. In contrast to the 'natural rights' interpretation of Locke when extended to IP, 'utilitarian' interpreters of Locke start from his attention to the investment made in the creation of things (physical and intellectual) but draw a stronger distinction between the potential for individual effort in making specific things and the interconnected nature of making mental 'things', both in their original creation and in the subsequent creation of new ideas thereafter. Utilitarian philosophers (such as Jeremy Bentham and John Stuart Mill) accepted Locke's base theory of property but sought to balance it against a defence of markets and the wider distribution of utility. As full property rights over an idea would give control of all applications of it, not just the individual and first version (in parallel to the making of a singular physical thing), utilitarian theory draws a radical distinction between property in physical things and a more limited conception of ownership in immaterial things. This utilitarian view was always dominant in the US, and its baseline distinction – such that IP be time-limited in most instances to prevent undue concentration of power – is generally accepted in law, even while IP holders continue to press (rather self-servingly) for what they think are their 'natural rights' for perpetual protection.

The Hegelian personality theory, in contrast, asserts that even if our book is extended a limited copyright protection, our names should remain attached to the work even after the copyright runs out. The Hegelian 'moral rights' model moves beyond simple economic considerations of IPRs. Using a Lockean analysis, IPRs are justified because they reward effort and/or if they strike the right balance between rewarding past efforts, allowing future innovations and enabling maximum utility of new ideas. For Hegel, a creation should always be seen as an extension of its creator's personality and hence carry their name in perpetuity. Whether emphasis upon balance or perpetual recognition in IPRs warrant differences over limited or perpetual economic control in creations/inventions or whether it is just a distinction between economic (payment) and cultural (recognition) as 'valuation' is another bone of contention. A follower of Rousseau would most likely conclude that all such attempts to legislate for who can and cannot use the products of the human mind diminish the common culture and simply enforce the interests of dominant actors.

KEY FORMS, RANGE AND DOMAINS

What then are the key forms of IP and what do these cover?

Copyright protects creative expression, covering textual, visual, musical and other 'works' (such as computer games and functional software). Copyright does not simply apply to 'fictional' work but protects 'non-necessary' form – a photographer's image of a landscape, or a historian's description of the past.

Copyright does not require registration. An expression must be fixed in a tangible form, but the law does not require an assessment of quality, only that it is the original expression of the author who fixed it. In other words, a copyrighted work does not have to be good, but it does have to be unique.

Moral rights associated with copyright protect the author's right to be named as author and to ensure the work in their name is not corrupted/distorted. Additionally, moral rights may mean that creators of works retain a commercial interest in the resale of original works. In France, resale of a painting sees the artist receiving a part of the resale value – unlike in, for example, the UK. The US does not fully recognize the moral rights of authors, despite provisions of the Berne Convention requiring signatories to do so.

Patent protects 'inventions' (although the discovery/invention distinction is as contested as the idea/expression distinction is in copyright). Unlike copyright, all patents require registration and are 'granted' by 'Patent Offices' that typically require applications to prove the invention meets specific criteria. Specifically, the invention must be non-obvious, novel and have utility ('that' it works, 'how' it works and what 'use' it serves). Unlike copyright, patent typically assumes 'progress' – not just novelty but 'improvement'.

Trademark is an IPR protecting brand images, associated logos, signatures, names, sounds, etc. Infringement of trademark is a form of counterfeiting – parallel to piracy in relation to commercial copyright infringement. Counterfeiting luxury branded goods is just that, while counterfeiting medicines and technical products most likely also involves patent infringement. Generic drugs however may infringe a patent but not the trademark. Trademarks, unlike other IPRs, can be perpetual.

Trade secrets may or may not be secret but refer to recipes and product particularities that would not be sufficiently technical to warrant patent protection, nor sufficiently creative to warrant copyright protection. Trade secrets relate to what makes a product distinctive and which is 'recognized' as stemming from a unique and traditional aspect of a particular maker rather than their competitors. The use of this IPR against 'industrial espionage' can become rife when free access to information is restricted.

GIs parallel trademarks but focus on place of origin in relation to the use of certain product names. Champagne is the most famous example of a product that can only carry that name if it comes from the Champagne region of France. GIs originated in European law and their globalization in recent years has been resisted by US corporations that prioritize universal copyrights and patents. This tension between IPRs as a defence of tradition and regional location against universal corporate ownership via global copyright and patent laws has been exacerbated by the extension of GIs as a defence of local, traditional and indigenous knowledge (commonly combined in the expression of 'traditional knowledge') by and for communities in the 'global south'.

Plant breeders' rights refer to IPRs that extend protection to strains of seed that have been selectively bred and hybridized. Such rights have allowed breeders to claim ownership over seed and hence to try and prevent replanting of seeds harvested from current crops. Such legal attempts to control farmers have been combined with more recent attempts to genetically engineer patented seed that cannot be replanted, but these things combined to produce a counter movement for *farmers' rights* which seeks to parallel the extension of rights to TK as noted in the previous paragraph.

Industrial designs cover a wide range of applied arts and manufactured objects deemed unsuitable for either copyright or patent on the grounds that 'designs' reflect more functional necessity than innovation relative to the pure arts or inventions. A chair has a number of functional characteristics that largely determine its design. Some countries (UK) offer no protection to stylized 'designer' furniture manufacturers, while others (Italy) protect 'style' much more, even in functional objects.

BINARIES IN DISPUTE

The notion of IP, then, embodies a number of crucial tensions that will be explored in the remainder of this work. These can be summarized as follows:

Between expression and idea. As has been pointed out, it is more than a purely abstract question as to where the distinction between expressions and ideas should be drawn. If 'expression' is loosely understood, such that anything with the look and feel of a prior expression could be said to be an infringement, then more control is given to the owner of the prior expression. Does, for example, any children's book about wizard schools infringe on Harry Potter? A strong demarcation between idea and expression, one which would make any difference between two manifestations of an idea sufficient to establish an independent copyright claim, would leave every expression unique and hence immune to claims to be infringing. Similarly, when designer labels use particular colours and words in association with their product, at what point does such visual content become 'theirs'? While drawing a line between where an idea ends and a specific expression begins can be problematic, abolishing the idea/expression distinction could allow the full ownership of the world of ideas to become a reality, which would be equally problematic. As such, you could not 'Just do it'.

Between invention and discovery. If an invention allows use of already existing, but previously invisible, objects, where does ownership end? Should the inventor just own the technique used to 'discover' these naturally occurring objects? Or, should ownership extend over the objects themselves? Whereas in the macro-world of continents and forests the invention/discovery distinction has been robustly maintained (in IP law at least – if not when modern farming techniques ideologically excused colonial land theft), in the micro-world of particles, genes and bacteria, recent legal decisions have fundamentally blurred this distinction. Rather, in parallel with owning 'ideas' through the undoing of the idea/expression dichotomy, patenting microorganisms makes it possible for IPRs to flow 'upstream' from the specific invention to the source – reality itself. Rights holders could own the world via owning ideas as manifested in naturally occurring objects that were previously unpatentable. Everyone else must now pay rent to stand on the shoulders of such giants.

Between monopoly and free-markets. While a capitalist society combines property ownership and free-markets, the two are not necessarily aligned. The promotion of free-markets requires regulation of monopolies, but protection of IPRs requires restriction on market entry through regulation of 'free' copying. IP protects non-rivalrous goods – those that have no natural scarcity because an expression/invention can be used by an infinite number of people at the same time without diminishing its functional utility. Free access to such non-rivalrous goods, however, would undermine the exchange value of such goods and so supplies must be limited to maintain a price. IPRs represent a suspension of free-markets in favour of monopolies in the interest of rewarding rights holders who it is assumed were motivated to innovate because they would be granted such monopoly rights. Such a control of markets may require additional interventions to prevent these monopolies from overly exploiting the suspension of competition. Free-market 'pirates' are a threat to IP concentration – to put it another way, such pirates bring lower prices to consumers labouring under the yoke of monopoly rents. Perpetual IPRs would indefinitely suspend markets and uphold IP at the expense of free-market competition. Imposing time-limits to monopolies reintroduces a possible ground for markets, but if IPRs are totally suspended then the benefits of property protection in enabling free-market entry may also be disrupted.

Between creators and the wider society. IPRs give protection to immaterial things that might otherwise be copied easily without limit. However, the vulnerability of immaterial goods – their ability to be replicated widely – which is said to warrant IPR protection is also what makes such protection so valuable (and potentially dangerous) if it could be achieved. The lock on your door protects far less than could be gained from owning rights over lock mechanisms in general.

Attempts to collapse IP into property in general (by whittling away at limits) parallel attempts to extend protection of expression closer and closer to basic ideas, collapsing discovery into invention and the neo-liberal prioritizing of corporate monopoly rights over price-regulating (i.e. genuinely competitive) markets (Crouch 2004, 2011). While IPRs are a social contract like any other property right, particular attention has been paid to the need to regulate rights over immaterial things because their unlimited extension (in time) would be so costly to the wider society (an unlimited monopoly on something that itself has no natural limits in its replication).

CONCLUSIONS

Global network capitalism is characterized by global flows and the transition from the primacy of physical goods to informational content as the key to value-adding profitability. As such, global deregulation of markets and global regulation of IPRs stand as the two reinforcing, if also contradictory, pillars of our current world order. The increased economic value of immaterial content, which parallels the devaluation of increasingly automated and interchangeable products and processes of production, is no natural effect of any 'post-industrial' or 'globalizing' logic as such. Technical automation could see immaterial content's economic value decline alongside, if not more rapidly than, the price of automated physical goods. Automation can just as (if not more) easily mass-produce films, music, chemical formulae and computer games as it can produce the cameras, CD players, bottles and consoles that might contain them (and very much does so). Fully deregulated global flows would see immaterial goods sold at free-market prices, prices which might well be very little indeed, if the same forces of deregulation as applied to labour markets and production regimes worldwide were applied to products of the mind. To some degree such free-market pricing happens in the form of free (but copyright infringing) file-sharing and live-streaming. It can also be found in trademark and patent infringing markets for 'knock off' designer goods, generic and counterfeit medicines etc. However, to the extent global network capitalism can remain dominant, it does so through the global regulation of property, including IP, while deregulating labour rights and global production networks. IPRs and their global enforcement are central to the ongoing domination of global network capitalism.

IPRs are social conventions that regulate access and use of the products of the human mind to promote/balance particular interests and must be studied as such. IPRs cover a range of immaterial content (from songs and stories to drugs and seeds). They take a number of forms (from copyright and trademarks to patents and breeders' rights). Their form, coverage and duration vary (between types, countries and across the years). In addition, finally, the rationales put forward to justify their existence, form and coverage are both divergent and contested. This chapter has sought to show that the very elements of the term itself, the notions of 'intellectual', 'property' and 'rights', are sites of dispute, not the foundations of any clear and natural basis for compelling assent to any particular regime. The centrality of IPRs in the global regulation of property, even while labour and production are deregulated, and the attempts by corporate lobbies and pliant states to present IPRs as naturally universal and absolute make it all the more necessary to bring such misrepresentations into question.

Where the boundary lies between expression and idea, between invention and discovery and between monopoly property rights in providing certain goods and the role of markets in allowing new entrants and price competition is neither natural nor necessary. Global network capitalism itself is riddled with both contradiction and resistance: between protecting property and promoting competition, between expanding markets via global networks and shoring up such channels against their alternative uses as conduits for highly 'efficient' free-sharing, and between an increasingly global regulation regime and the capacity of networked individuals to bypass both corporate intermediaries and harmonized regimes of control.

Chapter 2, on the history and globalization of IPRs in general, will develop this 'denaturalization' account. Chapters 3 (copyright), 4 (patents) and 5 (trademarks, GIs and design rights) will explore in more detail the specifics of ongoing disputes in these fields. In each case IPRs are shown to be central to contemporary global network capitalism's attempts to regulate property while deregulating labour rights and production regimes. However, at the same time each chapter highlights resistance to and contradiction within such attempts at 'owning the world of ideas'.

As this book will set out, since the end of the Cold War and through the creation of WTO and TRIPS, a new neo-liberal framework for global network capitalism started to be put in place. At the core of this new regime has been increased regulation (protection) of IP and decreased regulation (a reduction in protection) for labour. IP extension in duration, depth and geographical reach has been at the heart of all this, yet global circulation of people and ideas challenges IP control even as it also offers potential for greater profit. Digital networks similarly cut both ways, and protecting IP itself undermines free-market principles even while it does encourage unprincipled 'pirate' capitalism and anti-market sharing.

Just as the reality of global IP extension is fragile and contradictory, so also is the supposed justification for having IP protection at all. This book will highlight the weakness of claims that IP protection actually incentivizes invention and creativity more than it prohibits them and challenge the IP protectionists' argument that strong IP delivers maximum utility (overall benefits), an open and free culture, fair access to medicines, development enabling technology and/or environmentally friendly technology transfer.

As such, while significant elements of a global IP regime have been put in place, this regime is neither secure in practice nor defensible in principle. While IP protectionist lobbies remain well-resourced and influential players in business circles, the corridors of state and within international and global forums, resistance too is strong and growing, within both formal institutional arenas and in the alternative practices of those who simply bypass IP in their everyday sharing and purchasing.

Efforts at further roll-out of IP extension – in time, space and depth – continue, but such efforts have experienced significant opposition and have in some cases been defeated – at least in the short term. Beyond simply preventing further roll-out, some instances of roll-back have been achieved. Suspension and even abolition of IP in particular places and cases has also taken place (such as with generic drug licencing for essential medicines by some developing countries). One final scenario, prefigured in the everyday practices of many millions, is simply the withering relevance of 'global' laws in actually regulating the everyday lives of most people, not so much abolishing overextended legal protectionism but rather ignoring its claims – and being able to ignore them when such laws cannot be enforced. In this scenario claiming the right to own the world of ideas is just a very extreme case of global hubris. King Canute may have ordered the tide not to come in just to show that his law really did not govern reality. Our rulers appear to have no such modesty. Claiming to own the world of ideas they appear not to have noticed that their feet are getting wet, or if they have noticed they still believe they have the right and power to command that the tide turns back.

2
ORIGINS, HISTORY AND GLOBALIZATION OF INTELLECTUAL PROPERTY

Origin stories can be instrumental in understanding the underlying assumptions that have helped to construct a contemporary policy area. Identifying and understanding the history of the concept of IP is no different. In the previous chapter, we delved into the meanings behind the words intellectual, property and rights, as well as the tensions inherent in this idea. By investigating the origins of IP as a concept, we hope to shed light onto how this umbrella term that is used to refer to a wide variety of different legal regimes has changed over time. While the words themselves have a long history, their meaning has not remained stable but instead has travelled quite significantly as the scope and breadth of what we call IP evolved.

Today, as discussed in the previous chapter, IP is used to refer to a disparate set of practices associated with different technologies, countries and approaches to invention and sharing of knowledge. The term is often used interchangeably to refer to one of the many regimes it covers. For example, it is common to use the words copyright and IP to mean the same thing. Or, the term can be used to refer generally to any type of abstract property claim. It is not unusual to hear people refer to something as 'their intellectual property', though such references are made without any clear understanding that multiple possibilities as to what that property is might exist, nor does such a reference indicate an understanding of the complexities of how such a thing might be protected. IP broadly conceived is now even making its way into American national security discourses. US officials claim that foreigners are hacking into US systems and stealing what is referred to as American IP (Halbert 2014). Such use of language is political. Corporate lobbyists similarly claim their 'war on piracy' extends the 'war on terror' and the 'war on drugs' that characterized the decades' either side of the millennium (David and Whiteman 2014).

As IP has taken on more contemporary significance, the history of its emergence has become an area of scholarly focus. Today, a plethora of scholarship exists interested in mapping the historical terrain of IP, especially as it relates to copyright and patents. This scholarly investigation is multinational and multidisciplinary and uses a variety of techniques to better understand the history of IP so as to make claims regarding its contemporary meaning and policy directions. In this chapter we will first detail the origins of the concept of IP; then provide a brief history of the primary legal regimes this umbrella concept covers – copyright and patent law primary among them; and finally – but most interestingly perhaps – map out the rise of today's global IP regime, its power, structure, scope and yet also its limits and the resistances to it.

THE HISTORY OF IP AS A CONCEPT

As Susan Sell argues, the history of IP is not linear and is rife with contestation (2004, 268). The ongoing and historically nuanced debate about IP, as discussed in the previous chapter, is not *just* about whether IP is property but also, if property it be, what type of property it is. Some scholars argue that we should not call the limited rights extended to protect these types of creative work property at all (Smiers 2008; Boldrin and Levine 2008). Boldrin and Levine, for example, titled their book *Against Intellectual Monopoly* because they argue we should not conflate the concept of property with that of monopoly rights. That being said, the language of IP has long been associated with copyrights and patents, to the point that virtually all the literature on the subject uses the concept of IP as a general descriptive term. This does not mean, however, that the idea of IP *as property* should remain unchallenged or uncritically assessed. While the first chapter sought to deconstruct and critically interrogate the term IPRs, in this chapter we will look more historically at the concept.

The contemporary debate over IP, as Sell points out, is intricately linked to public policy. How we define this type of property will influence the balances struck and the policies defended. These theoretical beginnings were discussed in the previous chapter in terms of their Lockean and Hegelian origins. As noted in Chapter 1, Locke's account was taken in different directions by 'natural rights' and 'utilitarian' interpretations. While IP holders often revert to the natural rights frame when making a strong case for their 'rights', it is the utilitarian balance of interests approach that has been central to the framing of law, even if rights holding lobbies have also always been active in tilting the interpretation of any such balance in their own favour. A utilitarian account of IP focuses on its functional use in fostering mental labour rather than using claims to natural rights arising from authorship and originality as a justification for extending IP protection.

Such utilitarian approaches are most clearly exemplified in the emergence of the American system of copyright where protection of copyrighted works was offered to incentivize innovation by protecting the possibility to profit from the work. In contrast, the moral rights of an author to have his or her name associated with the work is an important aspect of French copyright law where the individual personality of the author must be kept central to copyright claims (Sell 2004, 272).

Justin Hughes in recounting the origins of the term IP suggests that the idea of creative work as property is not new, but has long been associated with copyrighted products, though they were originally designated as literary properties, not as IP (Hughes 2012, 1294–1295). Sell has found references to the concept of IP in the early 17th century (2004, 270). By looking historically at the concept of IP as it evolved in English, French, Italian and Spanish cases, Hughes finds that the term IP was used broadly to refer to a variety of different types of creative works (but still focused on copyrighted works) by the mid-19th century. Other related terms such as industrial property and literary property also remained in use. However, in all cases, by the mid-19th century the term IP was in general use (Hughes 2012, 1303–1310). Ecuador was the first state to enshrine the concept of IP in its constitution, which happened in 1845, primarily to focus on protection of patented inventions (Hughes 2012, 1310). The post-revolution Mexican constitution written in 1917 included the concept of cultural rights, one of the first constitutions to do so (Álvarez 2014, 281).

While calling creative abstractions property has a long history, the use of the term IP, according to Hughes, came to prominence with the creation of the World Intellectual Property Organization (WIPO) in 1967. While the precursor to WIPO, the Bureaux Internationaux Réunis pour la Protection de la Propriété Intellectuelle, did include the phrase IP in its title, Hughes argues that in reality the concept of industrial and intellectual property was largely interchangeable until WIPO helped consolidate the concept through its name (2012, 1297–1298).

By the mid-1980s, Hughes argues, the umbrella concept of IP was being used far more regularly to the point that other terms (literary property and industrial property) fell out of use (2012, 1308). Today, the concept of IP has come to stand internationally as an umbrella term that covers copyright, patents, trademarks, industrial designs and the like. The creation and evolution of IP as an umbrella term does not, however, mean that debate over the nature of this sort of 'property' has diminished. Rather, the legitimacy of IP *as property* has been a consistent part of the historical debate (Rose 1993). As pointed out in Chapter 1, there is nothing natural about the concept of property per se, as Mark Rose elaborates in his foundational work on copyright as literary property.

While John Locke's labour theory of property first gave literary men access to appropriate metaphors to define their work as property (Rose 1993), these metaphorical extensions from the physical to the literary – while taken as literal by some – were never fully taken 'literally' in law.

Thus, as those delving into the history of IP today have articulated, the road to the present was paved with numerous battles over the scope and breadth of these property rights. That being said, while resistance and debate have been integral to the evolution of the myriad legal doctrines under the term IP, the concept has only broadened out over time. In other words, once a new domain of knowledge is defined as 'intellectual property', which can either include a new innovation (like when computer games were invented) or a new genre of rights (like GIs), it is integrated under the larger umbrella of IP. The process of creating these property rights appears to go only one-way. Once a category of work is protected as a kind of IP, so far there have been no instances of depropertization. The expansion of IP brings additional types of creativity under the umbrella of a capitalist property rights regime. As capitalism expands it remains unlikely that a given creative category, once classified as open to own-ership, will revert back to a prior legally unprotected state. Individual works will eventually enter the public domain (although the term extension has pushed this 'eventually' ever further into the future), but to date the categories open for inclusion have not witnessed such reversion. So, even as we acknowledge the nature of the property right as a social contract, it is important to note that rescinding property rights once granted is far more difficult than expanding property rights to begin with. As we develop the specific histories of individual regimes, this process of propertization will become clearer (Löhr 2011). The way the concept of IP has expanded over time, despite resistance, is part of the historical story to be told.

Central to the origins and framing of all forms of IP law has been the tension between the ownership of the creation, which implies an ability to control its dissemination, and the desire for social innovation understood as an important element of human progress. Almost every author writing on the subject of IP has noted the constant and ongoing tension between individual ownership (and control) of ideas and the social nature of ideas. A particular version of romanti-cism presents creativity as the result of the inner workings of the detached and original genius. However, such constructions of 'romantic creation' as purely individualistic acts were only themselves a partial and largely distorted account of 'romanticism's' relationship to culture, community and nature (David 2006). Individual ideas do not exist in a vacuum, but rather emerge out of social inter-action and emersion in the general and specific flow of ideas. The social nature of creative work is important to acknowledge, and as such, our current legal structure does acknowledge that there must be a limit placed upon the right to control inventions and literary works. It helps that IP evolved as a function of the enlightenment, where progress and an unflagging faith in the construction of a better world through ideas were foundational to the policy-making process. To ensure progress, as the US Constitution notes, it is necessary to construct *limited* monopolies, thus acknowledging the relationship of the individual to the need for and value of social interaction within innovation.

As the history of IP is written, one of the significant questions to be asked is how well the extension of limited monopolies has done in sparking innovation. As can be expected, there are numerous answers to this question depending upon how the measure of innovation is framed. For example, Timothy Wu's (2001) excellent book about technological control and monopoly power details how innovation is often slowed by strong ownership rights. From an economic point of view, Boldrin and Levin (2008) have argued against patents as they hamper innovation. There are numerous concerns emerging from fields of creativity where the logic of IP is beginning to rear its head – fashion design, quilting and other material arts, cooking and such. These 'negative spaces' of IP, defined by Raustiala and Sprigman as creative industries that do not as of yet have strong IP laws governing innovation, continue to innovate. Yet the pressures to, and complexities of, creating new types of property rights are becoming more visible (Raustiala and Sprigman 2012).

In the next few pages of this chapter we will briefly discuss the origins and history of the myriad IP regimes and how these regimes are internationalized and extended across the globe. Each regime has followed a distinctive path into existence and covers different types of creative works. While we offer some of that history here, we will develop the specifics of these regimes in later chapters as well. The common threads that connect these legal regulatory schemes under the banner of IP are, first, that all these forms of protection regulate the double interface (a) between intangible idea/observation and tangible expression/invention, and (b) between tangible expression/invention and its physical embodiment or carrier. The tangible expression/invention sits conceptually between pure ideas/observations on the one hand and specific physical objects that contain/utilize the expression/innovative step on the other. A pure idea/observation cannot be protected by IP. IP applies only when such 'abstractions' are manifested in tangible forms (which are not themselves the same as individual physical objects as such). So, for example, prior to digitization, a novel was held in the physical print medium of a book. However, it was not the physical book per se that was subject to copyright laws but the expression contained in that object. Thus, you could sell your physical copy of the book or share it with others, but you could not make additional copies of the text and sell those. Thus, the property rights were divided. The person purchasing the physical book owned a property right to that specific copy, but the copyright owner retained ownership of the expression written in the book. Nobody was supposed to own the pure idea/observation. Today, tangible expression (that which IP covers) encroaches further and further up into 'ideas' and 'down' into physical objects themselves.

Second, laws were originally designed to protect commercial uses of these types of properties, which are otherwise very easy to appropriate (at least by rival manufacturers, publishers, etc.), given their distinct non-tangible nature. This non-rivalrousness, as mentioned in the previous chapter, required the construction of a legal regime to ensure adequate scarcity in what would otherwise flow quite freely. However, today, of course the law has gone well beyond merely protecting commercial uses and now includes all possible uses including derivative works based upon an original, small appropriations and non-commercial sharing.

HISTORY OF COPYRIGHT

With the introduction of the printing press in Europe and the ensuing radical transformation in the circulation of knowledge there, new concerns about copying and controlling the copy emerged. One aspect of the concern over printing, not typically recorded in the copyright narrative, was the government's desire to control what was printed and to censor that which the state believed should not be disseminated. The second aspect of the transformation wrought by the printing press was the growth of a market in literary works. In this context, commercial publishing could have an impact on the livelihood of both authors and printers, as could 'piracy'. Thus, literary property came to be regulated with commercial interests in mind alongside prior political interests in controlling the circulation of ideas. As conflicts between authors and printers and between 'authorized' printers and 'pirate' printers developed, legal debates over copyright reflected the concerns of the many interested parties (Rose 1993).

Most origin stories focus upon the 1709 Statute of Anne as the first copyright statute extending a limited monopoly to literary works (Ochoa and Rose 2002). While publishers sought a perpetual right in their products, the Statute of Anne only provided a limited term of protection, a decision that was upheld in the landmark case *Donaldson v. Beckett* (1774) (Ochoa and Rose 2002, 917). The Statute of Anne in the UK, its creation and contested interpretation, exemplifies the struggles over how to define ownership in literary products. These same debates became central to the construction of the US constitutional language designed to protect IP. As Ocha and Rose note, the framers of the American

Constitution ultimately settled on a utilitarian view of IP. As the framers understood it, these were not 'natural' rights but rather monopoly rights granted by government for a limited time. Even with these arguments in place, many in the newly formed US were deeply suspicious of the power of government to grant monopoly privileges (Ochoa and Rose 2002, 926–928).

What is interesting about copyright from the perspective of the present looking backwards is how far the idea has travelled since its inception. Establishing copyright over literary works was central to the original legal debates and statutes. However, it is now the case that far more than books are protected under copyright law. From copyright's limited initial goal – to protect booksellers (and note that it was booksellers, not authors that were protected here – as assigning ownership to the author was not to come until the mid-19th century) – the metaphor of ownership, or we might say the social contract, began its expansive journey. As indicated by the evolution of things covered by copyright under US law, expanding copyright to cover things other than books was part of the process of further owning the world of ideas (Association of Research Libraries 2014). The American expansion follows and has been followed by other countries in a very similar sequence, especially given the requirements associated with membership in WIPO and its associated treaties. Late to join the Berne Convention (only in 1988), the US was once strongly resistant to international copyright enforcement, which it saw as exerting 'Old Europe's' control over knowledge. Yet, once the US became the dominant player in the production and sale of such culture, it became the primary driver in attempts to expand and harmonize copyright worldwide. Today, American IP protection mirrors and is mirrored in the international agreements that defend copyrightable works worldwide.

The common denominator found in all forms of copyrightable works is that they are types of creative labour that can be 'fixed in a tangible form'. Once fixed, the law prohibits unauthorized copying. What also becomes clear is that copyright has evolved over time in reaction to technological innovation. As new technologies make new forms of expression possible, copyright law broadens to include more things. However, given the already existing assumptions about authorship and ownership, the underlying principles upon which copyright is based remain the same, even though one might argue that a computer program is a far different creature both creatively and commercially than a movie or a book. What connects all these things together – from sound recordings and architectural works to literary works and maps – is the fixation of the creative expression of an individual (identifiable subject/legal personality) into a form that can then be shared with others.

Despite the common requirement for tangible fixation, the diversity in copy-rightable subject matter raises significant concern. Michael Carroll identifies what he calls the uniformity costs of IP, when the law protects so many different things in the same way. Copyright law as 'one size fits all' has its own policy consequences. Many businesses and all end-users would be better served by specific, flexible and shorter legal terms, suggesting a need to rethink policy beyond one blanket copyright framework (Carroll 2005). Instead of expanding the ownership of ideas through perpetuating one broad and uniform instrument, specialized regimes for particular purposes might make more sense, especially given that the economic life of most copyrightable products ends many decades before the copyright does.

HISTORY OF PATENTS

Innovation and technological development in the world of patents, while sharing a common trajectory with copyright law, has a separate history. Often this lineage is traced to the guild system and the relatively secret methods used and carefully guarded by such a system. The earliest emergence of a patent system is traced to Renaissance Italy and the 15th-century Venetian system of protection for devices and processes requiring skilled labour and ingenuity (Duffy 2002, 710–711). From there the idea of patents spread to Germany and on to France and England, brought by Italian innovators as they travelled (Duffy 2002, 711–712).

In England, the precursor to the patent was the letters patent, designed to encourage trade and innovation in England. These royal decrees began in the 14th century as England sought to encourage foreigners to travel to the country, with a promise of monopoly protection for 14 years – the span of two apprenticeships to train people in their trade (Mossoff 2000, 1259). However, the first Anglophone patent law was the English Statute of Monopolies in 1624, though patents as privileges granted to inventors and craftsmen existed prior to that date (Biagioli et al. 2011, 25–26). The English state began granting monopoly privileges in the mid-1550s, but it was the 1624 Statute that was the first law that granted patents as rights secured for achievement rather than as privileges granted through favour. The act was passed to end what many saw as the political abuse of patent privilege by the Crown. The new law undermined the idea of a patent as a privilege and opened the way to patenting a swathe of new inventions, rather than just incentivizing the travel of old ones to England from abroad (Ochoa and Rose 2002, 912–913; Mossoff 2000, 1264–1265).

US patent law, much like copyright law, takes up the debates that the British model initiated. According to Mario Biagioli, the 1790 Patent Act passed in the US represented a conceptual break in how governments designed patent law. Prior to the 1790 Act, the privilege of a monopoly went to the person who put the invention to work first. Such a process focused on the local application of knowledge. The US Patent Act, in contrast, focused upon novelty in who thought of the idea, not where that idea was first reduced to practice (Biagioli 2011, 29–30). Shifting the focus of patents to novelty instead of practice produces a different type of focus for patent law. Such a shift, while seemingly insignificant, did as a matter of policy mean the workability of an idea became less central to its patentability claims than its manifestation in the form of something novel. Fast forward to the 21st century and the broad patents issued over novel ideas and the long-term implications of such a shift can be seen in patents for generic inventions with broad but as yet unused potential applications. We return to this issue in Chapter 4.

Central to both copyright and patent debates are theoretical arguments about natural rights, social contracts and utilitarian justifications for government-sanctioned monopolies, the philosophical foundations of which we discussed in Chapter 1. In both cases, what began as a government grant of a monopoly privilege by the Crown shifted into a different type of social contract entirely. Adam Mossoff argues that the transition between a royal patent prerogative and the understanding of patents as a property right negotiated within a larger social contract was made possible, in the UK at least, through the adoption of a natural rights approach to IP laws (2000, 1258).

As was the case with copyright, the scope and depth of patent law has expanded over time to include new forms of subject matter. So, for example, under contemporary patent law in many states one can patent a business method, a seed, a living organism and much more. While the limited duration of protection for patentable subject matter has not increased in the same way that copyright duration has expanded, many industries have found ways to continue to enforce their patents even after they have technically been terminated through a process called 'evergreening'. Thus, while not perpetual, patents have become a far more expansive and powerful form of legal protection than they were in the past. We will return to patents in more detail in Chapter 4.

HISTORY OF TRADEMARKS

Trademarks, as a form of IP, offer a different type of social contract between the mark holder and the general public than that found in patent and copyright law. In part, the difference is the result of who authors a trademark. While both copyright and patent law retains the legal fiction of an individual creative author and indeed the appropriate registration in both cases requires that the author/ inventor be named, trademarks are clearly the child of a commercial enterprise. Obviously, trademarks, especially modern ones, are the creative work of advertising agencies or company employees, but unlike copyright or patents, the individual authorship of such marks is rarely, if ever, central to their use or protection.

While other forms of IP offer a limited time of protection prior to entering the public domain so that these creative works or inventions can then be used as the scaffolding for new works, trademarks exist to assure the public that the product they are purchasing is from an authorized dealer. A trademark is a perpetual property right so long as the company that owns the mark uses the mark in conjunction with their products. A trademark may be believed to ensure the quality of a product by aligning it with its brand name. However, this is a misattribution (Chon 2014). The public may be protected by trademark enforcement from a dishonest business seeking to market its product under the name of a better known and more trusted competitor. However, trademark protection does not ensure that the 'trusted' brand is in fact trustworthy, only that they are the legal seller of a product carrying that mark, an idea we will return to in Chapter 5. Trademark regulates the identity of the seller, not the quality of the product or even the origin/originality of the producer (the design and manufacture of which is very often outsourced even as the corporation retains the 'brand'/'trademark'). Thus, while trademarks are considered an important kind of IP, their existence is not premised upon protecting the genius of an original author, despite the fact that, of course, this type of work can be quite creative.

Sandforth's case (1584) marks the first known legal case involving a trademark dispute (Stolte 1998, 507–508). The case involved a clothier who filed a complaint against a person who was marketing an inferior product under the same name as his own, a practice that ultimately hurt the plaintiff's business (Stolte 1998, 529–533). While the court did not find for the plaintiff, what is important about the case is that, according to Stolte, it is the foundation of Anglo-American trademark and an indication of the protection from trademark infringement as a common law right (Stolte 1998, 510).

While the legal history of trademark law predates the industrial revolution, trademarks gained popularity in the late 19th and early 20th centuries as factory-based manufacturing became more central to the production of goods. National markets meant the birth of national brands, and modern trademark law can be associated with the national marketing and distribution of products (Merges 2000, 2206–2207). Thus, while its roots also dig deep into history, trademark law comes into its own with the growing importance of advertising and mass marketing.

Today, trademarks go well beyond simply protecting a company name. Trademarks can include colours, sounds, phrases associated with advertising the product and any other possible aspect of a branding scheme that identifies a specific product. Trademark law is the foundation of what modern corporations sell – not simply a product but the brand itself. It is not just the product that a person is interested in purchasing but the image associated with these commercial goods as well. Thus, corporate branding instills trademarks and the law surrounding them with far more power over how we make our commercial choices than the legal category originally commanded (Klein 2009). As efforts are put into controlling 'non-traditional marks' such as shapes and smells, it is clear that much like other areas of IP law, the scope of trademark law has changed from its origins into something much broader today.

HISTORY OF TK AND ITS PROTECTION

The construction of IPRs as time and otherwise limited by necessity places some knowledge (sometimes from the start but otherwise eventually) outside the protection of law in what is called the public domain. Given that both copyright and patents exist for a limited time (though in the case of copyright this is quite a long time), it means that once the law ceases to protect the rights associated with the copyright or patent, the work becomes publically accessible without requiring permission from the owner to reproduce or use the work. A limited monopoly is extended to an author or creator with the understanding that the works will at some point be freely available for use by the public once the period of protection ends.

However, conceptualizing IP as limited and developing the associated concept of the public domain creates problems over how one ought to recognize the cultural significance of TK, traditional cultural expressions and other forms of creative and innovative work that have never been protected by modern IP regimes. It is often difficult to protect these other types of knowledge because they existed before and/or beyond commercially oriented western IP law, despite being appropriated and commercialized by colonial and corporate actors. Furthermore, the logic of the sole inventor or original author does not fit well within cultures where individual contributions are not recognized as separate from collective cultural survival. In some cases, such cultural processes are lost to history, and even if it would have been possible to locate an individual creator, those names are long lost. All cultural works that are no longer within the scope of IP protection are subject to appropriation and use without the authorization of a creator or a creator's heirs. Such work is within the public domain. The appropriation of indigenous peoples' knowledge from such a public domain by western commercial actors has led some to ask whether the logic of such a public domain works when balancing protection and access between different cultures rather than within the history of any particular society.

First, the collection of knowledge from indigenous peoples throughout the globe is closely aligned with the colonial projects of the European past. Colonization by western forces included numerous investigatory trips around the planet to collect plant life, animal life and people, including their cultures, in the name of progress and science. Such widespread appropriation could occur because western explorers did not conceive of indigenous peoples as existing in anything more than the state of nature. They were certainly not protected by the IP regimes systematically emerging to protect profitable knowledge in the west itself. Thus, colonization and the appropriation of indigenous knowledge have gone hand in hand (Smith 1999; Halbert 2014).

Second, as the concept of IP has taken hold and as different forms of IP have become more pervasive, the protection of TK has become an important issue in IP debates (Dutfield 2006; Oguamanam 2006; Sherman and Wiseman 2006; Graber and Burri-Nenova 2008; Boateng 2011). Given the widespread and continued appropriation of indigenous cultures by the west, one political approach to protecting TK from further exploitation has been the attempt to establish property regimes based not upon the individual contribution but on collective rights over cultural expression. While there is an uneasy fit between IP and TK, there is now an effort at WIPO to establish some method of protection that would align the needs of indigenous peoples throughout the world, and to value their cultures, with WIPO's mission to promote IP.

More recently, the advent of a new type of IP, GIs, has found resonance with indigenous groups. GIs of course move well beyond the protection of IP in TK and were developed in part to more rigidly protect products perhaps best associated with trademarks. Thus, the names of French cheeses and wines can be more clearly controlled based upon a regional marker of identity. GIs are a layer of property rights that build upon trademark in an individual brand. As a property right based upon a territory rather than an identifiable individual innovation, and designed to protect the commercial products of a region, the creation of GIs (like trademarks) create a different type of ownership in ideas disconnected from the original genius of any individual. Indigenous groups have found that such rights resonate, though not unproblematically, with historical cultural practices (Coombe et al. 2014a, 2014b).

THE HISTORY AND EVOLUTION OF INTERNATIONAL IP

The acquisition and spread of knowledge has been integral to national development and progress. As part of that development, intellectual and academic
exchange has long reached well beyond national borders, with early inventors
sharing their findings through publications and letters that traversed the globe.
While the pace at which such information could be exchanged was limited
by the transportation methods of the time, sharing knowledge is the foundation of the enlightenment ideal of progress. Furthermore, as people travelled
from one place to another, they brought with them their ideas and innovations. As discussed earlier in this chapter, one of the original justifications for
patent privileges was to provide an incentive for foreign innovators to share
their knowledge across national boundaries. Where ideas were not shared, they
were appropriated. For example, the 19th-century American approach to copyright was to unabashedly copy international works without paying the original
authors, an issue that became a central feature in copyright debates at the time
(Hughes 2012, 1328–1329).

Despite the colonial underpinnings that framed the global acquisition of
natural and cultural objects from around the world, such practices also indicate
that the flow of knowledge has long been global in scope. While the contributions of indigenous people was almost always appropriated into western
knowledge structures without attribution, the global appropriation of indigenous knowledge suggests that widespread exchange of ideas happened in
many directions (Smith 1999). Even today, western thinkers draw from the
political and social thought of indigenous people without attribution (zotofoto
2014). Fields such as ethnobotony and anthropology have begun to map these
exchanges and to make much more visible the global connections between
cultures, people, plants and their environment.

Knowledge does not respect the political borders of the nation. It is of course
possible with sufficient regulatory effort and enforcement resources to halt the
unauthorized production and distribution of knowledge-based products, such
as books, movies or pharmaceuticals. However, it is much less possible to stop
people from being inspired by seeing the works of others, or keeping them
from talking to each other, playing music together or viewing different types
of innovations. Today, from North Korea to the US the inability to control how
knowledge is shared via communication networks is seen as a new national
security threat. A recent report on the threat of IP theft concludes that foreign
students threaten American national security when they come to the US to
study and then return home with valuable IP inside their heads (The National
Bureau of Asian Research 2013, 13). These students may not steal tangible

items while in the US, but the government fears the flow of knowledge itself. The claim that getting an international education is now an act of IP piracy should seriously concern those interested in progress and innovation.

The literature available on the history and scope of international IP is vast (Ryan 1998; Drahos and Mayne 2002; Gervais 2003; Sell 2003; Yu 2004; May and Sell 2006; Bird 2008; Netanel 2009). Countries embrace nationalist discourses about innovation and cultural creation, where any innovation that occurs within their territory can be aligned with the nation-state. The state can derive a level of legitimacy for governance by aligning with the underlying cultural creativity of its people. However, the inspiration brought about by contact across national borders, cultures, languages and the like is not easily confined within the boundaries of the state system. As a result, laws promulgated at the international level are developed in such a way that signatory states can extend protection over IP beyond their own borders and thus beyond the sovereignty of their domestic law. Despite the fact that the law of a country stops at the border of its sovereign territory, the internationalization of IP protection means a country's 'intellectual property' continues to be secure as it travels the world. International IP law exists because ideas travel so easily across national borders and those who claim to 'own' these ideas wish to extend protection through the law further than the boundaries of their own state.

The earliest international treaties dealing with IP – the Berne Convention (1886) and the Paris Convention (1883) – were both negotiated in order to make domestic IP secure as it travelled the globe. Concepts such as national treatment, that a nation should treat the IP of another nation like they would treat their own, were developed to secure ideas and innovations that could otherwise not be controlled. Today, there are numerous international regimes focused on widening, lengthening and deepening IP protection. Central to the international negotiation of IP laws are the WIPO, and the WTO which is home to the TRIPS Treaty. Together, these agencies form the modern foundation for international IP laws.

In both cases, these agencies function under the auspices of the nation-state with negotiations taking place between representatives of the member states who have signed the agreements. In addition to the WIPO-administered treaties (most notably the Berne and Paris Conventions) and WTO TRIPS, other international organizations have an ongoing interest in how IP develops. UNESCO, with its focus on education and culture, has played a role in IP-related discussions and is home to the Universal Copyright Convention (UCC), signed in 1952 by the US and numerous developing countries who were unwilling or unable at that time to meet the standards set by the Berne Convention, in particular in regard to the enforcement of copyright on the works of foreign authors.

Specifically, the Berne Convention reflected the European approach to copyright law with a focus on the rights of the author, while the American approach was statutory and more limited and included notice and registration requirements not found in European law (Sandison 1986, 89–90). However, when the US agreed to sign the UCC it marked the end of US isolationism on issues of copyright, and many saw this treaty as paving the way for US membership of the Berne Convention (Sandison 1986, 90). The US finally joined the Berne Convention in 1988.

Once the Soviet Union signed the UCC in 1973, the treaty served Cold War détente purposes, being acceptable to both the US and the Soviet Union, an outcome that had taken numerous decades of negotiation. Having both parties as members of the UCC was completed in an effort to better secure the circulation of ideas between the US and the USSR (Levin 1983). When the Soviet Union signed the UCC, the US expressed concern that the Soviets were only signing to use copyright law to censor Samizdat works that were being published outside the Soviet Union (Johnston 1999, 123). Ironically, Cuba accuses the US of using copyright to stifle the spread of knowledge today (Álvarez 2014).

The Convention on Biological Diversity has also elaborated on the importance of IP for conservation work, specifically as this relates to plants and TK. Furthermore, Article 31 of the UN Declaration on the Rights of Indigenous Peoples states that Indigenous peoples 'have the right to maintain, control, protect and develop their Intellectual Property over such cultural heritage, traditional knowledge and traditional cultural expressions' (http://www.wipo.int/tk/en/resources/faqs.html#c2). However, there remains substantial debate over the relationship of IP to human rights (Graber 2008; Torremans 2008; Brown 2014).

WIPO is now home to numerous treaties that go beyond the initial protection of copyrighted works, industrial property and patentable subject matter. Today, there are treaties on the protection of GIs, also known as appellations of origin (Lisbon Agreement), phonograms and broadcasting (Rome Convention), audiovisual performances (Beijing Treaty), satellite signals (Brussels Convention), microorganisms (Budapest Treaty), access to publications for the blind, visually impaired and print-disabled (Marrakesh Treaty), and the not-yet-enforced agreement on integrated circuits (Washington Treaty). Since 2007, WIPO's larger mission has been framed by what is called the development agenda. WIPO's development agenda seeks the integration of development goals with an outcomes-based assessment strategy for WIPO programmes (Basheer and Primi 2008; de Beer 2009; Netanel 2009). The development agenda's 45 recommendations for action require WIPO to measure and report on how its activities facilitate development in the global south (Yu 2014, 113).

Along with development agenda issues, WIPO has also been involved in attempts to bring the protection of TK into the general sphere of IP protection and has supported the Intergovernmental Committee on Intellectual Property and Genetic Resources, Traditional Knowledge and Folklore. However, the protection of TK becomes problematic when WIPO's governing body only recognizes states as parties. Most indigenous peoples are governed by settler states that may or may not have their best interests in mind. The limit of an international system that only acknowledges states as legitimate negotiating parties is best illustrated by the gap between state power and indigenous communities. This gap in addition to the uneasy alignment of TK with mainstream ideas about IP has meant that WIPO's development committee has as of yet been unsuccessful in developing acceptable rules governing TK.

The WTO, replacing the previous General Agreement on Tariffs and Trade (GATT), has been a more forceful agent pressing for deregulation of international trade but tighter regulation of international IPRs. The creation of the WTO in 1994 (and enacted a year later) marks an international change brought on by the end of the Cold War and the rise of neo-liberal global network capitalism. Since its inception, the WTO has pursued a policy of deregulating global labour, trade and production regimes and of undoing regional and national barriers to free-market competition. However, the WTO also, as one of its founding acts, negotiated into being the TRIPS Treaty. TRIPS required all 161 signatories to the WTO to introduce into domestic legislation a requirement to uphold international IPR standards as developed in the TRIPS agreement. As such, while national monopolies and protections have been dismantled, global IPR monopolies and protections have been enforced and extended. Relative to GATT, TRIPS is backed up by tougher sanctions made available under WTO rules for punishing restrictions in the case of international trade and for punishing the non-enforcement of trade restrictions in the case of IP.

The emergence of the WTO and the TRIPS agreement created waves at the international level. Some commentators saw the TRIPS negotiation as a deliberate attempt to undermine WIPO's control over IP. As a 'forum shifting' effort, locating control over IP with the WTO was seen by some as an effort to bypass the myriad demands of the developing world, all of whom had a voice in the WIPO assembly but who had difficulty pressing for their interests during the TRIPS negotiations (Drahos 2003). The control exerted over the TRIPS negotiations by the US and other western powers meant that the language in the agreement favoured the developed world where already high levels of IP protection existed and where most IPR holders reside. The WTO more generally included a variety of trade issues of immediate concern to developing countries. IP was built into the foundations of the WTO, via TRIPS, as a concern of developed countries. It became a condition of joining the WTO that developing countries signed up to TRIPS. In exchange, joining the WTO offered developing societies some relief from prohibitive trade barriers on their goods entering the markets of developed states. Not joining threatened continued exclusion and marginalization. Most developing countries signed up feeling they had little alternative and no negotiating power over the terms of their entry. Implementation of TRIPS by developing countries was deferred for some years. The implications of the agreement were not therefore immediately clear. When implementation was required, around the turn of the millennium, resistance in the south intensified.

After TRIPS, WIPO negotiated the WIPO Copyright Treaty in December 1996, to which there are currently 93 members. This treaty was even more stringent in extension and enforcement than TRIPS. Christopher May (2007) suggests that immediately after the founding of the WTO/TRIPS treaty, WIPO sought to reposition itself as an agent ratcheting up global IP expansion relative to what WTO/TRIPS secured as the 'baseline' of global harmonization. Nominally UN agencies WIPO is funded by IP holders and the WTO by IP-rich states. While seeking to regain its position as primary agent for the IP holders that fund it – after losing out to the newly created WTO – WIPO sought to take a harder stance, but this led to further resistance from developing countries. In time both organizations (WIPO and WTO/TRIPS) saw resistance from developing country members, and this has led to IP lobby groups migrating in recent years towards bilateral treaties like the now-defunct Anti-Counterfeiting Trade Agreement (ACTA) and the ongoing TTP and TTIP negotiations to continue ratcheting up IP enforcement at a global level, even if not by means of global (i.e. multilateral) agencies and treaties.

Much has changed since the original TRIPS negotiations. As Daniel Gervais points out, TRIPS has moved through three phases. The first was the implementation (addition) phase (Gervais 2014, 101) through to the end of the 1990s, where signatories were pressed to sign into domestic law strong IP enforcement and harmonization. Second, there was a reactionary (subtraction) phase triggered by the controversy over the issue of access to medicine (Gervais 2014, 101–102). Access to essential medicine brought attention to the TRIPS agreement in the late 1990s and early 2000s when western pharmaceutical companies (and states) sought to prohibit the production of generic HIV/AIDS medications by countries throughout the global south. The issue of access to medicine became a lightning rod for the globalization of IP laws. The debate over access to medicine was a visible example for many that the neoliberal framework placed maximizing profits from pharmaceutical products, which were well protected under assorted IP laws over protecting human life.

Even if TRIPS included the necessary provisions to accommodate such emergency measures as producing generic versions of life-saving drugs (which some argued it did), pharmaceutical company litigation against developing states and lobbying within WIPO aimed to ensure this interpretation did not prevail, and that patented drugs stayed within their control.

For many states in the global south, a viable generic pharmaceutical industry allowed them to provide medicine at affordable prices for their people, and health care was conceived of as a human right. For western states or at least their powerful pharmaceutical lobbies, in contrast, access to medicine should only come through the preservation of a for-profit industry incentivized to test and distribute medicine by financial rewards. Western states, and their pharmaceutical industry lobbies, also claim that only monopoly-based prices generate sufficient profits to incentivize drug production in the first place (and into the future). As Chapter 4 details, such claims are highly self-serving, selective and exaggerated.

The tension between the developed and developing world sparked by the access to medicine debate initiated the Doha Round of TRIPS, culminating in the Doha Declaration in 2001. Access to medicine exemplified dispute over the neo-liberal approach to development, inequality, technology transfer and TK. At this point, the WTO began to encounter similar problems to those experienced by WIPO. Once developing countries came to appreciate the full implications of TRIPS, and built up some traction in opposing it, this multilateral forum became far less easy for developed countries to dominate.

While the WTO was negotiating the Doha Round and becoming a battle ground for international IP disputes, WIPO continued to be a forum for similar resistance to IP expansion from within the global south. Initiated by NGOs with an interest in development and member states from the global south, WIPO began to focus on its development agenda, a list of goals that if met will better align WIPO with the underlying mission of the UN to promote development. WIPO formally recognized its development agenda in 2007. These development-focused disputes create the conditions for a new phase in international IP protection.

According to Gervais, TRIPS has now entered a third phase, the calibration phase, where countries at very different stages of development seek to calibrate international protection with their domestic needs (2014, 102). We would locate the emergence of this third phase as arising gradually in the period between the TRIPS Doha Declaration in 2001 and WIPO's formal acceptance of its development agenda in 2007. This calibration approach would look more closely at the link between the local and the global and would allow (if implemented) different countries to create the types of IP regimes (strict or permissive) that best suited their level of development. This approach challenges attempts to foster a harmonized – strong, absolutist and universal – 'globalized' IPR regime and, as will be set out below, has led to the formation of alternative vehicles for dominant economic actors and developed states to pursue such ends for as long as WIPO and TRIPS remain open to a wider, democratic and open set of interests and voices.

Since 2007, the WIPO development agenda and its multiple development goals, multilateral IP negotiations have changed. Both WIPO and the WTO have had to come to terms with the fact that not all nations view the strong protection of IP as an end in itself. Attempts to align the protection of IP with the longer term goal of development have been proposed, but remain contested. However, even as WIPO and the WTO deal with development-related challenges to their primary focus upon promoting IP protection as the general good, other vehicles to cement strong IP laws with no room for nuance and manoeuvrability have been constructed. Many bilateral treaties, known as TRIPS plus, have now been negotiated with the US as the dominant negotiating partner, requiring many emerging economies to embrace IP regulations that go beyond those found in TRIPS. Most recently 'country club' treaties between a limited number of negotiating partners have developed to further expand international IP (Gervais 2014, 107). Agreements like the now-failed ACTA and its twin offspring, the TPP and the TTIP, alongside a number of others, show a retreat by the strong IP lobby from the multilateralism of WIPO and TRIPS. While WIPO and TRIPS sought to bind the whole world in one go, but then united large parts of that world against such attempts at global standardization, bilateral 'country club' treaties favour a more controlled negotiating environment (Yu 2014). What these bilateral IP-related treaties have in common with one another, and with previous multilateral treaties such as were brokered by WIPO and WTO, is that they seek to bind states within powerful legal regulative frameworks that limit the future scope of states to independently determine their own IP laws. That the (third) 'calibration phase' of TRIPS, noted above, moves away from TRIPS' original aim of creating globally binding legal frames above and beyond the control of states highlights that neo-liberal globalization was not inevitable and helps explain the shift by those seeking to further these original aims through a return to bilateral (sub-global) international treaties.

THE GLOBAL NETWORK SOCIETY AND INTERNATIONAL RESISTANCE

Manuel Castells in *The Rise of the Network Society* (2000a) argues that the global economy as we now understand it did not arise naturally from free-market forces, but was rather produced through the policy choices of governments and international financial institutions. As Castells notes, to function globally, multi-national corporations need the international structures produced by the WTO, including the TRIPS agreement. The examples above show that such global structures were initially negotiated by corporate and dominant states' lawyers and are difficult to renegotiate by less powerful actors, but such difficulties can be overcome, if often in only partial fashion.

Despite the success of global network capitalism as manifested through the network society, the same global network society has also placed in the hands of (now) billions of citizens the capacity to infringe IP as never before (regarding copyright and trademarks), just as attempts to protect IP in fact intensify the incentives and scope to infringe it (in relation to patents and designs). The global popularity of file-sharing sites is perhaps the best example of a networked and global flow of those things formally protected as IP. Sites like *The Pirate Bay*, Kim Dotcom's *MegaUpload* and his new encrypted service *Mega* are examples of the global flow of IP not yet controlled by copyright owners. Literally billions of downloads from people living in all parts of the globe show the popularity of accessing movies, music, video games, pornography and any other form of digital content on demand and in formats that can be used instantly.

File-sharing has continued to develop, suggesting that even with changes in the law that have sought to bolster IP protection there is a continuing movement in how people acquire cultural products towards free-sharing. State actors have continued to crack down on file-sharing sites and impose criminal sanctions on individuals who file-share. Yet, such efforts appear both futile and misguided given the culture of and the capacity for file-sharing that is emerging. File-sharing has grown as its practice has found ever more complex ways around the law. Increasingly 'distributed' modes of sharing have consistently removed whichever bottleneck within the latest sharing network was being targeted by the courts. While these targets were being removed, so sharers have also systematically undone all the technical encryption and surveillance devices being used by rights holders to lock down content and/or track down infringers (David 2010, 2013). Recent scholarship looking at the motivations and morality of file-sharing suggests complex and nuanced attitudes towards the purchase of cultural commodities and the relationships that are forged through sharing (Larsson 2013; David and Whiteman 2014; Whiteman 2014). Sharers reject the dominant legal frames and have the capacity to act upon such rejection. The law is bypassed both culturally and technically.

There is at one level a political economy of file-sharing where many users see clearly the distinction between supporting an artist and supporting an industry that is exploitative of artists. Even more complex is the way that those engaged in file-sharing perceive their media-sharing habits (Edwards et al. 2014).

It is not the case that those who file-share never purchase copyrighted content, but they do so in different ways now that they have the option to preview and select what they may or may not then purchase. It may be that someone will watch a movie they downloaded for free and then based upon that viewing go see it at the cinema (David 2013). It may be that they listen to a downloaded song and then hear the artist live (Krueger 2004) or purchase related music. In other words, those involved in the sharing of cultural products remain involved in an economy where they purchase media content. However, media industries seek to control the circulation of cultural goods in absolute terms. All unauthorized use or access is deemed 'piracy' and 'theft'. Every possible viewing or exposure to media content is seen as requiring 'purchase'. Such an absolutist paradigm leaves no room in law for the sharing-based media consumption habits of a global file-sharing community. On the other hand, in practice, the law's lack of room to accommodate sharing has not stopped such free circulation of content.

The global resistance which has developed in response to efforts by states and multinationals to secure more restrictive IP laws through trade agreements negotiated by states on behalf of economic interests without public comment or transparency highlights that the global network society is not a one-way street. For example, when the ACTA was being negotiated, the talks were held in secret, with only trade association groups having access to the government representatives developing the rules. However, once made public, people took to the streets in protest (Lee 2012). Such protests were global in nature, spanning multiple cities, especially in Eastern Europe, where ACTA was felt to be reminiscent of Soviet-style surveillance (Kirschbaum and Ivanova 2012). In part, resistance to ACTA was spurred on by the global protest hacker collective *Anonymous*, itself a manifestation of the global network society. While ACTA sought to ensure better security for copyright and trademark holders over their products, the existence of popular revolt highlighted the global divide between states negotiating for corporate interests and the interests of the people living in these respective states for broader access to knowledge and products protected by IP law. The resistance generated by ACTA helped clarify that corporate interests and state officials' support for such interests are not synonymous with the needs of citizens. When protests led some state actors to withdraw from the process, the ACTA negotiations collapsed.

Protests continue against the ongoing negotiations surrounding the TPP and the TTIP, two bilateral transnational agreements that picked up where ACTA left off. TPP and TTIP also seek to enhance IPRs for large patent and copyright holders and, much like ACTA, demonstrate the gap between global economic interests protected by western government negotiations and the interests of everybody else (Baker 2014). While ACTA was genuinely global, TPP and TTIP are only transnational when taken individually, but are global when taken together. These agreements are designed to bypass national legislative processes and impose even more restrictive IP regulations on signatory states, even as states will be required to act in enforcing their conditions.

CONCLUSION

The history of IP continues to be written. As IP becomes more globally relevant and academically significant, scholars have turned towards examining its historical origins in more detail by investigating how the law plays out in individual cases and more broadly as part of an ongoing social contract between different social actors. Retelling the larger story of IP origins situates the present within a more clearly understood and political past. Such a process helps reveal the fact that the laws we have today, protecting all forms of IP, are neither neutral nor the product of unanimous consent. Rather, the history of IP is a history of political battles, theoretical disputes and, of course, an interest in monopolizing and controlling markets in intangibles.

For those suspicious of IP extension, however, telling the history of IP is important because it shows that there has always been resistance and debate over what justifies/fails to justify protection of IP. In addition, as has been pointed out in this chapter, a historical account of IP clearly shows that terms of protection and grounds given for protection have diverged over time and have differed between places as well as between different forms of IP. The debates over international IP are no different – while TRIPS may have been implemented initially without significant global resistance, such resistance is now part of every international debate over IP.

Divergent terms of protection between countries, over time and between forms of IP, highlight the non-existence of any discernible 'natural' or 'necessary' assignment of an origin of ideas (as required to found claims to natural rights) whether to protect individual 'author' claims against society's appropriation or to balance relative claims of individuals and the wider community. Similarly, the different claims as to what warrants protection in ideas – promoting individual 'originality' in the case of copyright and patent – in contrast to promoting the preservation of established forms in the case of trademark, GIs and TK – force us to recognize the non-existence of any singular, or natural, foundation for assigning property rights in ideas. The specifics of this historical debate should not be lost to the overarching and prevailing sentiment that IP is somehow a natural right, or that the individual should be rewarded more substantially than the larger cultural and social world within which that person works and is inspired. Ongoing debate at the international level over how far and how best to protect IP also signals the social construction of these rights which, far from being natural, were initially imposed on the global south.

The rise of IP over the last three centuries has culminated in the last three decades with an attempt at global IP harmonization alongside radical expansion in reach, duration and depth. Powerful lobbies have sought to shape the formation of older and new institutions at the international level. To some extent they have been very successful. However, resistance and failure has also been their lot. In the following three chapters these struggles to extend and resist global IP harmonization and intensification are documented as they relate to the most significant fields of IP, copyright, patent and trademark (with related discussions of GIs and industrial designs). There have been victories and losses on all sides and in all areas. There is no singular and definitive outcome, even as a mapping of the terrain enables a clearer understanding of what is at stake.

3
COPYRIGHT CONTROVERSIES TODAY

Despite its intended purpose – to protect the creators of works of authorship – copyright fails to protect the vast majority of those working in the creative industries today. Even those who earn royalties from copyright are most often worse off than if they were earning wages for the manual/physical performance of their art. Predominantly, copyright acts to protect large IP holders, namely publishers, broadcasters, record and film companies, etc. However, the contradictions of global network capitalism and resistance from an increasingly globalized and networked citizenry bring security for even the largest IP holders into question. New technology allows the ease of free circulation, and halting such circulation requires aggressive, largely futile and counterproductive surveillance, legal and educational campaigns. What this chapter hopes to clarify is that the construction of a global copyright regime infringes more rights than it protects, offers only tenuous technical and legal security and alienates customers even as they find new ways of 'voting' with their feet. While global network copyright industries continue to develop apace (the commercially facing digital revolution), so too do a range of contradictions and resistances (in particular a sharing-oriented digital revolution). In this chapter it will be shown how copyright law has been extended geographically, in depth and in duration in recent years. As we will describe below, two global digital revolutions face off against each other, with no certain outcome in sight.

GEOGRAPHICAL EXTENSION

As we discussed in Chapter 2, the earliest copyright laws (from 1709 on) were national in origin. The 19th century saw states in Europe adopt and expand copyright law, but these laws not only differed by country but were of limited significance in claiming protection outside the rights holders' own country

(May and Sell 2006). The US built copyright protection into its constitution, but early American legislation did not extend such protection to works produced abroad. The mid-19th century saw some European countries abandon copyright even as others were legislating for it (Johns 2009).

The Berne Convention for the Protection of Literary and Artistic Works of 1886 was the first international effort to protect literary property (a term that has now been replaced by IP) and required signatories to uphold the rights of creators from other signatory countries as they would for their own citizens. The treaty also barred the requirement that authors 'register' works to gain protection. However, by 9 September 1886 there were only eight such signatories: Belgium, France, Germany, Italy, Spain, Switzerland, the UK and Tunisia (WIPO 2014). From the outset the treaty was managed by an office in Switzerland, and, now managing Berne and a raft of other treaties, this office has morphed into today's WIPO – based in Geneva. According to WIPO (2014) the Berne Convention now has 168 signatories. Most Western European states joined in the decades after 1886. The US did not join until 1988, China not until 1992, the post-Soviet republics later still, and many developing nations after that (though some joined earlier even before decolonization in certain cases).

The accession of the US to Berne in 1988 marked a significant shift in US engagement with global copyright enforcement. While once a colony resisting 'Old Europe's' cultural dominance, the US is now the primary beneficiary of global copyright extension (Vaidhyanathan 2003; May and Sell 2006; David 2010, 42–57). China's accession to Berne in 1992 and the accession of post-Soviet nations to the WIPO-administered treaty marked the near completion of copyright globalization.

As a former colony, deeply hostile to the early use of Crown Copyright to enforce censorship, the US, having turned from being poacher to gamekeeper, is now the leading nation in pressing for geographical harmonization, as are its leading IP-rich 'creative industries'. In addition to the US's leadership in multilateral multiextension treaty negotiations, in recent years the US and its corporate sector have driven a range of bilateral free trade and IP-related treaties between the US and less powerful trading partners that further press copyright protection in space, expansion in scope and extension in time (Yu 2014).

The geographical extension of copyright has happened both nationally and globally. International protections shape and then reshape domestic law as each country's copyright laws must be expanded and enhanced to meet the new global benchmarks. However, expansion of copyright geographically is not the only way copyright has taken on broader dimensions.

DEPTH EXTENSION: LOOK AND FEEL

Copyright extension is not just about geographical extension. Since the Berne Convention was initially signed, it has been updated seven times to allow new forms of creative media to be included (photography, film, television, digital content, etc.). The early film industry adapted novels for the screen with copyright impunity as the text was not seen to be infringed by its visual expression (Vaidhyanathan 2003; Lessig 2004). Plays adapted novels similarly. Lawrence Lessig (2004) gives the example of *Mickey Mouse*. First created as an animated parody of Buster Keaton's (1928) film *Steam Boat Bill*, Walt Disney's (1928) *Steam Boat Willie* (which first introduced Mickey Mouse) was a 'hack' protected by 'fair use'.

Today, copyright law is far stronger in prohibiting copying on the basis of 'look and feel' rather than requiring something that would be mistaken for the original. While authors and musicians have always played with similar forms to create distinctive 'takes' on chord progressions, rhymes, narratives, characterizations, genre styles, etc., the combination of geographical extension (see above) and time extension (see below) with tougher interpretations on how close constitutes copying and a more relaxed interpretation of what is sufficient to receive protection (these later two being mirrors of one another) creates a deepening of copyright.

Global copyright holding corporations lobby for favourable legislation nationally and transnationally. Once such legislation is passed through transnational treaties, the circle is closed by advocating for further reenforcement nationally. These actors are then able to press for favourable interpretations and enforcement in court, often against alleged infringers who cannot afford to defend themselves. Even in the event of failure in a lower court, the ability to afford appeals makes success a 'poker match' where the deeper pockets of large rights holders perpetuate themselves. In business this is referred to as 'litigation through the margins' (Phythian-Adams 2014, 37). Big firms calculate that they can keep fighting a case until a smaller rival runs out of money and has to 'fold'.

Another way copyright is extended is over how originality is assigned and how aesthetic judgements are made. John Terhanian (2014) notes how, despite the fact copyright law precludes judges from using aesthetic criteria (of quality) when evaluating what should and should not have copyright protection, these have crept into the law anyway. In the recent case, *Cariou v. Prince*, the judges used measures of financial value and artistic status to determine if the artist being charged with copyright violation was indeed guilty. The wealth and status of the 'appropriation artist' Richard Prince was taken by the court as evidence enough of his being a creative and hence 'true' artist. Despite Prince's acknowledgement that he had used Patrick Cariou's photographs in constructing his own work, Prince claimed his addition of bars and lozenges over the original images constituted a creative act. The court's judgement listed Cariou's weak sales and prices as evidence that he was not a successful creative artist, relative to the millionaire Prince. On this basis the court rejected Cariou's claim that Prince's use of his images infringed his (Cariou's) originality and hence breached copyright. As this case demonstrates, powerful actors can draw upon the work of less powerful actors without such appropriation being judged infringement, as distinct from when an artist is accused by another artist backed by a more powerful commercial (postcard making) actor – as was seen in the case of *Rogers v. Koon* in Chapter 1. Economically successful actors are more successful in enforcing infringement claims against less successful ones than the reverse. While access to the courts generally is contingent upon access to wealth, court determinations then use wealth and commercial success as a proxy indicator of 'true' originality.

TIME EXTENSION – NEAR PERMANENCE?

Over the last 300 years the duration of copyright has stretched. Tyler Ochoa (2010, 156–165) outlines both extension and convergence. Pre-copyright, the monopolies granted to stationers in 16th-century England, were effectively per-petual, but the stationers acts under which such protection was granted were themselves time-limited. Non-renewal of the act in 1695 created the space into which copyright emerged with the Statute of Anne in 1709 (covering the newly created UK). This gave a 14-year protection and a possible 14-year extension if the author still lived. In 1814 protection was changed to 28 years or life (if longer), and in 1842, 42 years or life plus seven years if longer.

Pre-revolutionary France offered six-year protection terms that could be repeat-edly extended, changing in 1777 to 10 years or life if longer. Post-revolutionary change saw life plus five years and then life plus 10 years in 1791 and 1793, respectively; life of author or widow plus 10 years in 1810; and in 1866 life plus 50 years. Prussia offered life plus 30 years in 1837, and this became the standard for the subsequently unified Germany in 1871. Germany matched France in 1934.

The US converged in its constitutional convention and early copyright law (1790) around the English figures of 14 plus 14 (if the author still lived), moving to 28 plus 14 in 1831 and 28 plus 28 in 1909 (assuming author sur-vival in both cases). The US followed Berne's life plus 50 in 1976 (though not then yet a member). While the original Berne Convention (1886) followed the

French model, Germany's life plus 30 and France's life plus 50 differed. This was resolved by accepting the lower figure as the baseline. Berne's Brussels revision in 1948 saw life plus 50 adopted as the baseline. In 1993 the EU raised its baseline to life plus 70 years, which was matched in the US after the 1998 Sonny Bono Copyright Term Extension Act.

'PROTECTING' THE 'CREATIVE INDUSTRIES'?

Copyright extension across space, depth and time mirrors growth in production, internationalization and significance of immaterial creative works, but, of course, granting and extending such protection itself contributes to the expansion of international markets for such goods and hence their value. The standard economic argument for granting copyright in the first place is to incentivize creative production, or at least to incentivize the circulation of such creative work (Phythian-Adams 2014). However, as Litman (1991) observes, most writers and musicians, when asked, have little idea how copyright actually works. It is unlikely therefore that they are 'motivated' to create by copyright as such. Instead of inspiring creation, Phythian-Adams notes, the commercialization of such works and hence their wider circulation may be incentivized by the prospect of controlling sales. Such commercial actors, so the standard economic model goes, themselves fund (by means of advances and royalties) creative artists.

It is the control of the resulting works by these commercial actors that makes copyright relevant. David (2010) outlines the claims made by such intermediaries and their lobby groups. These groups claim that without the prospect of revenues generated by control over access to copyrighted content, there would be no investment in creative artists and, by extension, no creative work (BPI 2008). Edwards et al. (2013) document how successful such lobbyists have been in persuading governments of their claims, even while being equally unsuccessful in persuading audiences of this case. In fact, as David and Whiteman (2014) show, the 'piracy' label has been accepted as both true and negative by legislators, while audiences have embraced the term as a positive identity.

To justify the necessity of copyright, IP owners claim they must have such control in order to afford future production. When looking at copyright and music, Andrew Kirton (2014) notes that intermediaries operate in what they claim is a high-risk environment. Such risks also hold true for film, television, literature and computer games. For music, it is argued that 90% of records do not 'recoup'. Failure to 'recoup' is when an artist's royalties are insufficient to repay the upfront investment made by their label. Record labels and other copyright-based creative industries claim they need to take the lion's share (85–95%) of net income to cover the cost of those releases which do not 'recoup'. As such, royalty rates hover between 5% and 15% of net sales income. Albini (1994) and Love (2000) point out the deception underlying this account.

Artists are given a small royalty on the premise that the publisher/label needs to recover investments on the authors/artists who do not 'recoup'. However, the label/publisher 'sets' the cost of any advance – a little paid directly to the artist to live on, but mainly paid out for production time, legal and management fees and/or promotional costs – against royalties that will be only a fraction of the full net income generated. The artist is thereby required to repay almost all the investment made in them out of a tiny fraction of the revenues their work generates. Records/books fail to 'recoup' not just because of poor sales but because of how small a proportion of revenues the artist is assigned and from which such a high proportion of costs must be repaid.

A one million dollar advance, spent over two years eating and paying producers, managers, lawyers, video makers, tour bus drivers, sound engineers, etc., may lead to an album that sells a million copies. Retailing at $10 each, the net return to the record label is $6 per record. If the artist then gets a (very rare) 15% royalty, that would be 90c times one million ($900,000), still less than the million advanced. The artist would still owe the record company $100,000! The artist failed to 'recoup' even when the record company, retaining the other 85%, made $5.1m. On their balance sheet the record company had to 'subsidize' their artist's failure, leading to reducing the artist's royalty rate next time. While most records fail to recoup, and most artists end up owing their record companies money (David 2010), record companies still make profits – even from many of the records that do not 'recoup'. The small number of records that do 'recoup' mainly leave the artist breaking even, but make very high profits indeed to their labels.

Dave O'Brien (2014) extends this account to the 'creative industries' more widely. Over recent years, publishers, record companies, broadcasters, computer software and gaming companies have pressed hard for IP extension on the premise that IP protection protects what has become central to 'post-industrial' societies in the age of 'global network capitalism', i.e. the buying and selling of immaterial goods. In presenting the case for such extended protections, copyright holders (and related IP holding lobbies) equate the interests of copyright holders with those of all people involved in the 'creative industries'.

Governments across the developed world (and beyond) have accepted the lobbyists' argument that protecting creative property protects creative workers. O'Brien highlights that in fact increased regulation of IP protection in the creative industries has gone hand in hand with increased deregulation of employment conditions in those same industries, such that most of those working in the entertainment, leisure and arts sector experience increased insecurity even as the interests of IP holders are more tightly secured. The indebted musicians who will owe money to their record company even after their record makes their label a substantial profit are just the most extreme cases of the new economy of precarious (but 'creative') labour that O'Brien describes (see also Ross 2009). Royalties, rather than wages, mean work with no security, no set hours and often rewarded well below any legal minimum wage levels if they exist.

Copyright and royalties, rather than employment and wages, leave most working for nothing. Indebtedness for actually producing creative work parallels and combines with increased indebtedness for study and unpaid internships for a generation 'freed' from the securities of stable employment and career in the name of securing property rights. While the aspiring star with a million dollar advance is held up as an ideal within this new economy, Steve Albini, when noting the reality of such prospective debt bondage, concludes, be careful what you wish for: 'Some of your friends are probably already this Fucked!' (Albini 1994: online). Only a tiny fraction of authors and musicians make any money from the copyright in their work, and of these only a dizzyingly small fraction make the equivalent of the minimum wage from royalties (Holmes 2003). Most musicians make what money they make from live performance (Krueger 2004; Krueger and Connolly 2006). Most writers teach, talk, work for hire, present or otherwise 'perform' live to make a living. Most actors and dancers make their living from live performance, not royalties on recordings.

Rather than the structure established by the recording industry, another business model exists. Free circulation of copyrighted material increases publicity and increases the money in audience pockets. Alan Krueger shows ticket sales and prices rise because of online copyright infringement. The digital threat to copyright industries benefits creative workers. The rise of film downloading has not diminished attendance at cinemas as previewing encourages public attendance. Even as free-sharing has decimated the video rental market, new streaming alternatives have risen to offer consumers alternatives they are willing to pay for even when they have the choice to download or stream for free. Despite efforts of the recording industry to hold onto their old business models, such efforts are really a form of protectionism. While some modes of distribution may die, others will form. The destruction of the mechanical form of music (and entertainment more generally) distribution is not the end of entertainment itself.

PROMISE AND THREAT IN GLOBAL NETWORK CAPITALISM:
THE FIRST AND SECOND DIGITAL REVOLUTIONS

The three paradoxes of IP manifested within global network capitalism, as outlined in Chapter 1, are at their most extreme in relation to copyright. Capitalism has always contained the contradiction between regulating property rights and deregulating markets, but IP-rich goods place property rights in the good being sold, not just in the machine producing it, and hence intensify this paradox. Digital networks increase market opportunities and reduce costs, but if distribution becomes uncontrolled and price falls to nothing, such efficiency threatens capitalism. Globalization has seen the rise of transnational IP-rich corporations, yet it also empowers individuals to bypass these distributors and share directly. Copyright protects creative expression, and it is such creative expression, whether in the form of literature, music, film, television or computer software, that is most fully informational. Physical books, records, newspapers, videos, cables and the like, once the essential delivery devices for copyright-protected content, can now be bypassed by anyone with a network computer. Just as global network capitalism revolutionized the creative industries through digitization, this first (IP-centred) digital revolution is also challenged by a second (IP-evading) digital revolution.

The first (commercial) digital revolution occurred in music and then moved out from there. The compact disc launched in 1982 (David 2010, 32), replacing vinyl and largely replacing cassette tape as the medium for selling recorded music. The period from 1982 to 1999 saw the largest and longest profit boom in the history of the record industry (Sandell 2007). Digital recording, processing, compression, storage and distribution reduced costs, while prices rose and reformatting saw back-catalogue sales rocket as well. It was a perfect storm. As Sandell notes (2007, 30), record companies were too busy printing money to worry that in releasing music in digital form they were in effect giving away their own master copies.

The second (sharing) digital revolution also began in music. Cheap, mass-market CD burners in the mid-1990s caused a little alarm (Krueger 2004), but it was the fusion of the MP3 compression format, internet distribution and Shaun Fanning's search-and-share software 'Napster' in 1999 that ended the profit storm and ushered in an era of crisis for record companies, alongside the huge growth in live performance and hence pay for musicians. Closed for contributory infringement in 2001/2002 (David 2010), Napster's legal Achilles heel (its central server) was removed in later, fully peer-to-peer services. Prosecution of uploaders shifted the technology to encourage torrent services where files are downloaded from multiple uploaders (each only providing a fragment of the file and hence unprosecutable). Attempts to target downloaders led to streaming services where viewers watch or listen but do not 'download' a copy (David 2013). Legal (David and Kirkhope 2004), technical (David and Kirkhope 2006) and cultural strategies (David et al. 2011; David and Whiteman 2014) to contain the second digital revolution in music have all failed and promoted the development of even more fully distributed forms of sharing (David 2010).

Parallel histories unfolded in relation to film, journalism and recorded television; digitization has revolutionized each of these sectors. Initially reducing costs and increasing profits, digital content when combined with internet distribution reduces reproduction costs to zero, and, in abolishing scarcity, the second digital revolution opens up existential challenges to copyright-based business models. Copyright industries were the initial ones to experience the first and second digital revolutions, and within that sector recorded music was in the vanguard.

The most recent sector to feel the impact of the digital revolution is live sport. Live sports broadcasting started migrating from analogue (terrestrial) television to digital satellite broadcasting around a decade after music's migration to the CD (Kirton and David 2013). Monopoly rights over live sport and global distribution deals swelled the finances of early adopter digital broadcasters and allowed the emergence of new global media players, such as Rupert Murdoch's News Corporation – with its Sky, Fox and other specific manifestations (David et al. 2014).

Manuel Castells (2009) charts the rise of such global network media corporations and how they combined digital affordances, the post-Cold War opening up of new markets, with new global IP regulations in the 1990s to create truly global business empires. Nonetheless, just as digital television was a decade behind the CD, so a decade after the rise of Napster, internet broadband speeds and streaming channels first made it possible to freely distribute online what was previously controlled by law and by the need to have dedicated cable or satellite delivery (Birmingham and David 2011; David 2011; David and Millward 2012).

PROTECTING COPYRIGHT BY INFRINGING FREEDOM OF EXPRESSION, CREATIVITY AND HUMAN RIGHTS

Copyright provides virtually no reward and no protection to the vast majority of creative producers. 'Paying' royalties rather than wages reduces working conditions and rewards for most. Mass online copyright infringement reduces record sales leaving audiences with more money for live events thus making performing artists better off. Protecting copyright from sharing defends capital in the 'creative industries', but it does not defend creative workers and indeed threatens them, as it does audiences and the wider population.

Ian Brown (2014) documents how far attempts to defend copyright infringe upon other rights, such as to privacy, freedom of expression, the right to access and participate in the general culture, and to education and learning. Copyright defenders have actively lobbied to have copyright recognized as a fundamental and universal human right. If copyright were to achieve the status of a universal human right, Lillian Álvarez (2014) argues, developing countries must either suspend such claims or remain unable to provide their citizens with fundamental educational and cultural resources. Chris May (2006) makes a similar point regarding open source software in developing countries. In seeking to enforce restrictive copyright laws, high levels of surveillance are demanded. Governments around the world have legislated to require internet service providers to reveal personal details of account holders to copyright owners if their representatives claim a user's account display suspicious behaviour that 'might' be the result of copyright infringement. Such 'suspicion' of copyright infringement, unless by entrapment (itself unlawful), remains unproven by the copyright owner, but subsequent threats made to such 'suspects' based upon these unproven claims may generate payment of fines that amount to intimidation and extortion.

One example of such tactics is documented by Dave Wall (2014) who describes the case of ACS Law in the UK and its practice of 'speculative lawyering'. The law firm used a provision in the UK Digital Economy Act (2010) to gain single court orders to demand the personal details of 10,000 internet users per order on the pretext that these accounts had linked to sites which ACS Law claimed made unauthorized copyrighted content available. That ACS Law could know who linked to such sites suggests the possibility that the sites themselves were 'honey traps,' sites established to lure possible copyright infringers in, but this is unconfirmed. If not by such an unlawful method of knowing, any such claim to know remained deeply suspect. ACS Law then sent demands for £500 to each person if they wanted to avoid legal action. Many paid up out of fear before the indiscriminate ('speculative') nature of the scheme was declared illegal. The practice has since migrated from music to pornography and from the UK to many other jurisdictions.

Another way in which extension of copyright terms has a chilling effect on the creative process occurs when more and more creative content is covered long after the author's death. Wordsworth's concern for his extensive family (Marshall 2005) spurred him to write and campaign for copyright extension for seven years after the author's death. Today's term of 70 years after death of the author rewards corporate back-catalogues, venerating yesterday, not the creation of anything new. Claudy Op den Kamp (2014) addresses how the length of copyright intensifies the problem of orphan works. With such long terms of protection after an author's death, an increasingly large array of content now has no clearly identifiable rights holder in part because unregistered copyright does not require the rights holder to present themselves until they (might) wish to make a case for infringement. The problem is compounded by the fact that it may be unclear who the rights holder is. A grandchild, business partner's grandchild or some other person unknown could come forward and demand punitive compensation for infringement 100 or more years after a work's production. This means that film and other archives housing creative work now contain vast quantities of material that nobody is prepared to release or make use of for fear of being sued. In the name of near perpetual veneration of past creation, such orphans are buried, just as works with known heirs remain legally incarcerated. The cultural commons and our collective memory are radically diminished. Online circulation, while potentially unlawful, limits this diminution. However, not everything is digitized yet.

EMPOWERING CREATIVE PRODUCERS, AUDIENCES AND FAN COMMUNITIES: THE NEW COMMONS

As will be discussed in Chapter 5 (on trademark), global network capitalism's IP paradoxes are exemplified in the mirroring of corporate outsourcing of production (and globalization of distribution) by commercial 'pirate' counterfeiters and a culture of 'piracy' where consumers demonstrate they are willing to buy symbols detached from 'authentic' production and product. In the case of copyright, far from promoting a counterfeit capitalism, the rise of global network sharing is as much a challenge to criminal free-marketers selling counterfeits as it is to copyright holders. Global digital networks empower the end-user to directly circulate informational content. As has already been noted, free circulation of formally copyright-protected content reduces opportunity costs (money spent on recordings cannot then be spent directly on concert tickets) and promotes fan attendance at live events for which performers are better paid than by royalties. Digital networks also foster fan engagement through fan fiction, fan cultures, user-generated content, open source and creative commons licenced co-production and self-regulation, as well as the kind of 'sharing' piracy exemplified by political 'pirate parties' rather than commercial 'pirate' businesses.

The empowerment of fans and other creative users is one of the important manifestations of the global circulation of culture via digital networks. Raizel Liebler (2014) helps identify the importance of these interactions by exploring the multiple worlds of 'fan fiction' circulating online, with a particular attention to comparing East Asian (Japanese and Korean) and western (US and Western European) legal and corporate responses. In Japan and Korea, fan fiction is more widely regarded as a legitimate form of expression and one that complements and promotes the commercial forms being emulated, copied and modified. In the west, copyright holding firms are more suspicious of fan emulation and are keen to promote a pacified conception of fandom (something to which Natasha Whiteman's 2014 work draws attention). Such attempts at pacification however are either ineffective or counterproductive. Liebler offers interesting counterpoints to legal regulation, firstly the creative responses of authors down the ages to fan appropriation/infringement – the most famous being part two of *Don Quixote* where the hero announces he is not going to go where the first book said he was headed and in so doing discounts all the copyists who had written erroneous versions of 'what happened next'. As Whiteman (2014) suggests, fans feel very much a part of the creative process and in many respects are. Seeking to prohibit their experiments with characters, stories and forms only diminishes the creative stimulation of their interaction with the artists they remain more than willing to reward, even while being happy to bypass corporate intermediaries where possible.

Beyond fan fiction, the question of user-generated content raises other complications within the paradoxes of global network capitalism. Greg Lastowka (2014) explores the dilemmas of user-generated content in relation to computer games. Early games were simple, free and non-networked. As such they were neither eligible for copyright protection nor were they profitable, and they were not widely circulated. Increasing sophistication, graphically, in narrative development and in the quality of 'game-play' created scope for copyright protection, while migration from science labs, through arcade machines to home computers (which were later increasingly networked) expanded both sales and the scope for infringing copies.

Two points of interest derive from the intersection of copyright and computer games. Firstly, scope for copyright depends on the 'game' being more than just a game. Game rules are not open to copyright protection, while creative works are. It has been hard for courts to decide whether particular code within a game is generic or a unique 'original' piece of programming, so emphasis has been placed on 'narrative', but games rely on 'play' as much as 'following' the plot. As games became more sophisticated, the very thing that made them open to copyright claims has also led to users claiming ownership over particular things they create within the game. User-generated content can be traded (and counterfeited). To the extent that game creators want to claim their game is more than just a set of rules and is in fact a unique 'work of art', they are vulnerable to this self-same claim from the very players of their games who argue the game is just the rules, and they the users have created unique stories and characters through these rules.

Secondly, despite claims to be suffering great losses at the hands of counterfeiters, games manufacturers have grown rapidly within the entertainment sector, overtaking music and film in revenue terms (Kirkpatrick 2013). As the purest 'digital' content, one might expect the games industry to have suffered more than music and film, not least because the gaming arcade appears not to have enjoyed any kind of revival on a par with live performance or even the revival of cinema in the age of digital downloading. It might be imagined that computer games (and software companies more widely) would be most radically dependent upon copyright for their survival, being fully digital and having no alternative 'live' or live proxy (such as going out to the cinema) income stream.

Yet, the opposite is true. Totally vulnerable to 'piracy' and non-commercial sharing, games companies have simply adapted their product to keep their audience paying. While the PC replaced the dedicated game's console in the 1980s, the 2000s saw the revival of the dedicated console on the premise that it promised better graphics. Game players chose to pay because they were being offered improvements, not because it was impossible to get PC versions. Games companies regularly update their products to make counterfeits of last year's version unprofitable.

The newest permutation of games includes online interactive versions, via central server hubs, which allow companies to exclude those using unauthorized copies. It is perfectly possible to find and use infringing copies, but millions choose not to. Games companies, unlike companies selling content that – while now digital – predated the digital revolutions, do not live on their back-catalogues, or even by stretching out the shelf life of current products by means of legal protectionism. Rather they constantly create new products people are willing to pay for (Langshaw 2011).

It is no coincidence then that the free and open source software movement, while largely antithetical to the hypercommercial character of some of today's leading games and software manufacturers, also shows how creativity is best fostered not by controlling past achievement but rather by constantly adding new things to what has already been achieved. Jyn-An Lee (2014) highlights the fact that large parts of today's digital economy depend upon non-proprietary forms of free and open source software (not least the internet and World Wide Web themselves), and that such models of innovation and development have proven more flexible, integrative and robust than locked-down proprietary forms. A simple illustration of this phenomenon lies in the repeated failure of Apple's Fair Play encryption when set against the collective actions of hackers (David 2010, 90–91).

The ongoing failure of copyright defenders to develop any form of digital rights management that open source hackers have not been able to unpick is another demonstration of the power of open versus closed systems. Anne Barron (2014) is right to offer a note of caution regarding the watering down of many of the principles of free and open source culture within the more legalistic 'creative commons' (cc). Specifically, she argues that the weaker versions of creative commons are not much different from copyright, yet the de facto free circulation of pretty much all de jure copyrighted content represents a substantive creation of a quite 'real' creative commons, even if the lawyers who drew up the concept remain bound to the legacy of the very 'permission culture' they sought to escape.

In response to the perceived need to better articulate a culture of sharing, the Pirate Party was created. Liza Dobbin and Martin Zeilinger (2014) chart the rise of 'pirate parties' as the political manifestation of this substantial culture of sharing. The Pirate Party International grew out of a small act of resistance to the global efforts to take down the internationally popular file-sharing torrent tracker service The Pirate Bay (TPB). In response to the Swedish government's prosecution of TPB, the Pirate Party was born (Falkvinge 2012). Since its birth, the Pirate Party has been remarkably successful around the world, now boasting over 60 national parties and seats in the EU and several European governments. While a minor party, the very existence of a political party dedicated to the reform of IP laws points to the sea change that has happened. While laws have been and continue to be promulgated at a global and transnational level to enhance the protection of IPRs, these laws now meet with a globalized resistance and a small but emerging political party that is focused on questioning the global expansion and prioritizing of IPRs relative to wider human needs and freedoms. Economic resistance – at the level of free-sharing and discounted generics – and cultural resistance via the same technical networks that afford dominant cultural and economic flows are therefore now joined by new forms of political participation.

INDIVIDUALIZATION OF ENFORCEMENT

Conflict between English and Scottish booksellers led to and followed on after the Statute of Anne, the first copyright law. Conflict between UK and US booksellers continued long after that (Johns 2009). What those accused of piracy in the book trade had in common with those selling copyright infringing sheet music, then recorded music, and then films, right up until the late 20th century, was that copying required a significant investment in fixed and variable capital. 'Pirates' were businesses albeit ones pressing free-market principles beyond the law. 'Piracy' was framed in law to address commercially oriented copyright infringement. The audio tape, on reels and then cassettes, the Xerox machine and video tape all made private copying possible and a perceived threat to copyright holders

(Marshall 2005), but digital network sharing makes the non-commercial copy a more serious threat to copyright holders than commercial pirates ever were.

The Berne Convention refers to piracy, but as the predominant form of piracy at that time was commercial, there was no distinction drawn between commercial and personal copying. Similarly, the UK's 1906 Copyright Act addressed commercial piracy as the only form, and this remained the case for the 1988 Copyright, Designs and Patents Act (Alexander 2007). TRIPS explicitly addressed 'piracy' as copyright infringement for commercial gain. For this reason WIPO's Copyright Treaty (1996) addressed digital distribution that makes non-commercial sharing far easier and hence more challenging to copyright holders. The 2011 ACTA (between the US, EU, Japan and Switzerland) sought to make non-commercial sharing a criminal offence, even while many signatories (and others) have subsequently diminished charges that can be levied against individual uploaders and downloaders, placing emphasis upon commercial actors providing advertisement-funded sharing networks. In 2012, after large-scale protests, the EU representatives to the ACTA negotiations refused to ratify the treaty, and as such, it has never been implemented.

What is the most disturbing trend, but one deemed essential for the future ownership of ideas in an age of empowered network individuals, is the punitive focus on the individual sharer rather than commercial 'pirates'. As it becomes increasingly obvious that the fans themselves are the problem for monopolists in a world where digital materials can flow freely, the legal apparatus being constructed to halt such flow requires increased individual surveillance and more draconian measures with which to threaten people. Such regulation makes internet service providers and other institutions responsible for turning over their users' identities for possible sanction. Colleges, for example, when requested to do so must identify for copyright owners students accused of downloading. These students are then sent cease-and-desist letters and often kicked off their college networks, which are among other things vital for their education. Such practices of surveillance and punishment have encouraged the migration from download services to streaming sites which do not require the user to make a copy and hence violate *copy* right (David 2013). The use of courts to require internet service providers to block access to streaming sites has simply led to the rise in use of virtual proxy networks and onion routers (Brown 2014), technologies initially designed to enable free communication in politically repressive regimes, but now used to circumvent control in economically repressive ones. Attempts to equate copyright violation with student plagiarism rather fell down as it was pointed out that colleges actively encourage students to use libraries without paying, exactly what they do when downloading songs from the internet for free (David 2010, 104–106).

CONCLUSIONS

The interconnected world of global network capitalism affords both the new transnational media firms that press to regulate copyright longer, deeper and further, and the non-commercial networks of individual sharers that challenge them. Copyright law, which was once the preserve of inter-firm rivalry, is now being revised and applied to regulate the interactions between individuals, though the success of such attempts in practice remains limited. How copyright will evolve in the future remains to be seen, but as its scope has broadened geographically as well as conceptually, the future copyright battles will continue to pit corporate copyright owners against possible users and other creators. If the notion of IP becomes more widespread and more people begin to see their creations as their property, it is likely that there will be more battles between competing private rights claims, even as further disputes over the balance between private protection and public rights carry on apace. However, the emergence of political parties such as the Pirate Party, who oppose the threat posed by too much property regulation in the digital era, combined with the massive public and worldwide resistance to the most recent efforts to enhance corporate property rights globally, suggests that efforts to keep cultural creativity open to sharing, either legally or 'illegally', will remain on the agenda.

Global network capitalism is confronted by its own contradictions and by a global network society that seeks to extend global and digital affordances in ways that challenge a prioritizing of IP protection worldwide even as everyone else is pressed into greater competition one against another. IP extension by geography, look and feel, and over time confronts sharing that is everywhere, total and instantaneous. What is good for corporations is not good for the creators they claim to represent, and artists find common cause with audiences in resisting IP and engaging in new ways or in more direct (if older) ways (like live performance). Protection of IP involves the infringement of more rights than it upholds, and even the claim to be promoting and protecting creativity folds when sharers routinely outclass proprietary products, whether in arts or in computer programming. Even as global network capitalism erects a global infrastructure to protect its interests in controlling IP, it finds its worst and most powerful adversaries are its own individual consumers – empowered to bypass them by global networks and increasingly annoyed at being both ignoring as citizens in the formation of IP legislation while at the same time increasingly targeted by such laws.

4
PATENTS AND TRADITIONAL KNOWLEDGE

The WIPO defines a patent as 'an exclusive right' granted for an invention, which is a product or a process that provides, in general, a new way of doing something, or offers a new technical solution to a problem. To get a patent technical information about the invention must be disclosed to the public in a patent application (http://www.wipo.int/patents/en/). TRIPS sets as its minimum standards that patentable subject matter must be 'new, inventive and capable of industrial application' (Leong 2014, 665). As these definitions suggest, a patent can cover a product, which is the outcome of the invention, or the patent can cover the process of doing something, often known as a business method patent. Patents can be extended to cover software, and there are numerous technological areas where patents and other sui generis forms of property rights protect a specific product, such as semiconductors and seeds. In both cases the definitions of what is patentable leave open the concept of what constitutes an 'invention' (Leong 2014, 665).

The standards for patentability are much more stringent than those required for copyright. Copyright law is written so that the creative (or aesthetic) merit of a work is not at issue. The law attempts not to judge good or bad writing, painting, photography or the like (aesthetic judgments do, however, inevitably seep into the law; Tehranian 2014; Suthersanen 2014). Despite this seepage, the law is not intended to make aesthetic judgements about a work, but only to ascertain that the work is original in the sense that it is not copied too closely from another work. For a patent to be granted, the invention must be both novel and better than what went before. In other words, there remains much more flexibility in copyright law regarding what is original than what can be claimed under patent law.

Patents also require a formal assessment of the progressive originality of the supposed innovation relative to all prior art. Patents have to be registered, something that the Berne Convention explicitly prohibits in relation to copyright, where claims need only be asserted in cases of dispute. The need to demonstrate substantive difference in claiming originality is much stronger and upfront for patents than is the case for copyrights. If a patent application is successful, the patent secures for the inventor a far more absolute and rigorous protection, albeit for a more limited time, than would be the case with copyright. A patent expires typically within 20 years of the filing date. However, during its existence, the patent, as the WIPO definition suggests, extends an exclusive right to the inventor. There are no fair use provisions for patents and any use of the patented invention requires authorization from the inventor.

The Paris Convention for the Protection of Industrial Property (1883) initially included 10 contracting parties, but today has 176. The Paris Convention is governed by the WIPO and covers patents along with trademarks and industrial designs, GIs and other aspects of what is called industrial property (WIPO 2015a). In order to streamline international patent processes, the Patent Law Treaty was concluded in 2000 and came into force in 2005. While it is open to all member states of WIPO, to date 36 countries have signed the agreement (WIPO 2015b). To seek international patent protection, a patent must be registered in every country where the patent owner wishes to assert his or her rights, but the Paris Convention gives the patent owner the right of priority, meaning that if the patent is registered in one of the member states, then the patent owner has a specified amount of time to register that patent in all other member states. WIPO houses a patent clearinghouse mechanism that allows for an inventor to streamline the patent application process internationally.

There remain some variations in the law globally, especially surrounding specific technologies and products. As we will discuss in more detail later in the chapter, some countries, for example, defend their right to produce generic pharmaceutical products as important for public health (Millaleo and Cadenas 2014). Others seek better access to technology through compulsory licensing or technology transfer (Rimmer 2014). That being said, all countries that are signatories to TRIPS and the Paris Convention adhere to a minimum standard of patent protection for inventions.

The patent system as currently constructed applies equally to all patentable inventions, but it has been argued that requiring countries, especially developing countries, to implement a uniform patent policy equally applicable to all industries might be suboptimal (Gervais 2014, 101). In this chapter we will sketch some of the controversies and current issues surrounding global patents and the way they help (or hinder) progress. We will discuss some of the areas of patent law that have had significant repercussions on the everyday lives of people throughout the world, have become the foundation of entire industries, or at least the foundation of their litigation strategies, and have raised patents to global visibility.

PROBLEMS OF PATENTS

Patents are intended to describe in some detail the scope of the invention as it is reduced to practice. As patents have become a more significant part of securing valuable business assets in a system of global network capitalism, the system as designed has become subject to several policy failures. One of the more significant concerns where patents have taken on economic significance is abuse of the patent system by people termed patent trolls. The patent troll takes two different forms. The first is someone who has applied for and received such a broad patent that most downstream innovation is infringing. This patent is then used in litigation against others innovating in the field, even if the original and broad patented object has never been reduced to practice. The patent holder is enriched through the general claims made in the patent and a willingness to sue others seeking to innovate.

Another dimension of such trolling practices is the creation of patent thickets. Patent thickets are designed to make entry into a specific field of innovation virtually impossible, thus functioning to depress competition and choke off 'upstream' innovation. Patent thickets are not a new phenomenon. Thomas Edison learned the practice in the late 19th-century US railway business, where buying up small tracts of land along the prospective routes of forthcoming railway lines allowed purchasers to then 'extort' exaggerated prices for those tracts from the rail companies who were seeking to pass through. Edison went on to take out over one thousand often highly generic patents (most famously on light bulb filaments, film spools, sound recording devices and in early electronics), many of which he did not in fact 'invent' but was only the first to register (Vaidhyanathan 2003). He then sought to monopolize both 'downstream' sales and 'upstream' innovation. In today's global network capitalism, strong patent enforcement stands accused of creating just such 'thickets', especially in pharmaceuticals, as will be highlighted below.

The second type of patent troll is a company or individual who did not invent anything but acquired the patents to a technology or innovation by purchasing them, often from a bankrupt company. Such people have a legal interest in defending the patent for money and see the patent only as a valuable commodity, not as something that might help produce 'progress in the arts and sciences'. They did not invent anything themselves, nor are they intending to use the patent to produce a product. To this type of troll, the patent is simply a legal tool used to exact money from others producing products in the same field. As business actors learn to game the patent system, there is increasing concern over the role patent trolls play. Their actions, while legal, undermine the intent of the law – to provide an incentive for invention and a limited time in which to recoup the cost of such invention. It is of course worth mentioning that while one intended goal of the patent system is to produce a marketable product, there is nothing in the patenting process itself that assures the invention will make its owner a profit. It only secures the right to exclude others from trying to do the same.

While patent trolls are one of the recent concerns raised by the law, the foundation of patents themselves is often subject to critique in the way it individualizes invention and reward and provides an incentive to privatize the results. Much like copyright, patent law tends to emphasize the inventive and lone genius, without recognizing the collective processes that underpin innovative work. Patent applications require an inventive step, meaning that the invention must be something new. However, the law tends to ignore that in many cases an inventive step is taken by an inventor because s/he is using already existing ideas in the public domain or what is often described as the 'heritage of humankind'. When speaking about copyrights and patents, that which has fallen out of protection is considered to have entered 'the public domain,' an idea we discussed in Chapter 2. However, given that lots of what could have once been potentially patentable or copyrightable inventions or creations either pre-date the law or were never protected under these western legal regimes, there is much that has been invented and created that has till now remained outside protection. Drawing upon what is termed 'the heritage of mankind' (or humankind), mining old knowledge never claimed as property to develop supposedly novel steps and hence new patent claims is therefore deeply problematic. As we will discuss below, while domestic laws (such as US patent law) can protect against patents being claimed on already existing knowledge in that country, that same protection does not extend to using the already existing knowledge that might be found in other countries.

Such heritage of course, while not commodified under the law, also does not exist in a vacuum. Examples in areas such as ethnobotony and pharmaceutical research illustrate the problems most clearly. In both cases, knowledge that has been known to indigenous and/or local communities for centuries is turned to as a source of new patentable subject matter. As a result of using such knowledge without attribution, controversies have emerged within the field of patentable subject matter over the line between public knowledge and that which is then appropriated as private via the patent system. The appropriation of what is called the 'heritage of humankind' into the commodified system of IP demonstrates the pull of owning the world of ideas that is central to the argument of this book. While such ownership is as of yet not perpetual and many tensions and paradoxes remain, the underlying pull is towards understanding human inventions as commercial and commodified, not as part of a larger and uncontrolled public domain.

As western scientists travel the globe seeking out plant materials with medicinal properties, they often tap into the knowledge of local communities to do so. The ensuing feelings of exploitation and the ways in which a collective body of knowledge has become appropriated and privatized has led to accusations of biocolonialism and biopiracy. Beginning with Vandana Shiva's polemical accounting of the networks of exploitation associated with patents to the far more nuanced body of work that has emerged to highlight the problematic relationships between TK and modern IP systems (Shiva 1997; Dutfield 2006; Mgbeoji 2006; Sherman and Wiseman 2006; Antons 2009), it is clear that an uneasy relationship exists between TK and the modern IP paradigm. A desire to seek a remedy for the exploitation of TK has led to innovation within the IP sphere. Some types of IP, like the use of GIs discussed in Chapter 5, seek to extend protection to communities as a whole over what might be identified as their cultural heritage. Other examples include efforts to use patent law itself to extend protection over TK.

One example is the Indian Traditional Knowledge Digital Project (TKDP). The TKDP will document the vast stores of local and traditional knowledge in practice throughout India as prior art. This documentation, it is hoped, will inhibit attempts to appropriate such knowledge for private patenting purposes (Thomas 2014, 363–364). Such a database is needed because of the problems of international appropriation and to better make claims regarding the prior art. So, for example, in order to secure a patent one must also conduct what is called a prior art search to ensure that the invention does not already exist. However, in the US, the rules governing prior art searches specifically exclude knowledge 'known or used' in a foreign country, thus significantly expanding the type of TK that could become subject to US patent law (USPTO 2014). Thus, while WIPO works to globalize patents through their patent process, the US has designed for itself a caveat to the global extension of prior art to the degree that it can more easily appropriate knowledge from around the world without acknowledging these appropriations. Within this global context, the TKDP database may not prevent appropriation by foreign corporations that only accept globalization as a one-way street (extending their interests). However, it will make such appropriations clearer and hence more open to scrutiny and challenge.

In the aftermath of global controversies over several visible examples, including the Hoodia plant discussed below, large multinationals have had to be more careful about their appropriation strategies and have also become more involved in the creation of benefit-sharing programmes that will acknowledge the contributions of holders of TK. However, these strategies are not without problems. Concern associated with benefit-sharing schemes for patented products based upon TK is exemplified by the difficulties of determining how best to allocate possible profits in the commercialization of the Hoodia plant. The San people(s) of Southern Africa have known about and used the Hoodia plant as an appetite suppressant for centuries (Darch 2014a, 265). As such, when the plant was commercialized and a global cry of biopiracy was levelled against the companies seeking to produce a diet drug from the plant, efforts were made to develop a benefit-sharing system. The problem became with whom to share the possible benefits of commercial success. First, it is difficult to actually locate the geographic origins of a 'natural' plant or process given that, as Graham Dutfield has pointed out, much of what is now considered to be 'local' flora, cuisine and culture has itself migrated there in the relatively recent past, whether by accidental or deliberate human intervention or by 'natural' processes (Dutfield 2014, 652–653). If current placement of a plant that has become integrated into TK is the result of prior displacement, then it becomes equally difficult to identify who to attribute first knowledge of that plant's properties to. Dutfield highlights the added difficulties that 'San' communities are dispersed across six states, and that non-'San' communities also claim Hoodia use as part of their 'traditional knowledge'.

Additionally, there are disputes over 'San' identity that must be worked through (Coombe et al. 2014b). There is no single voice or authority to speak for and act on behalf of the San claim. Finally, in the case of Hoodia, a patent claim was already held by the South African government's Council for Scientific and Industrial Research. The complexity of patents and benefit sharing play themselves out in this example. The attempt to produce a diet drug for a global market based on local/traditional knowledge accentuated controversies over the exploitation of this local indigenous community as diverse 'local' actors fought first for a share of this global market value and, secondly, among themselves for shares of that share. The scheme did not resolve such exploitation or disputes over it, but rather only raised new questions and concerns as the benefit-sharing scheme was put into practice.

Problems emerging from the framing of patentable subject matter as proprietary knowledge extend well beyond the concerns of appropriating the heritage of humankind for private gain. The patent system itself is based upon an important distinction between products of nature which cannot be patented and products that are the labour of individuals. To those fully entrenched within the legal patent system, it is the labour invested in the production of an innovative product that is relevant. To that end, the San would not deserve any monetary remuneration from the product developed from the Hoodia plant because they use the plant as found in nature, not as synthesized in a laboratory. While a diet product may have been derived from San knowledge of the Hoodia plant, the synthesized laboratory version is not the same as the original plant growing in the wild. Similar claims regarding the 'invented' (and hence novel) character of artificially synthesized/isolated forms of previously naturally occurring materials are also at the heart of claims over the ownership of living organisms and DNA sequences. We will further elaborate on these contemporary patent issues by examining the biotechnology revolution and its relationship to patents.

PATENTING LIFE AND THE BIOTECHNOLOGY REVOLUTION

Most scholars chart the beginning of the biotechnology revolution to the landmark US Supreme Court decision in *Diamond v. Chakrabarty* (Burger 1980). In the early 1970s, Ananda Chakrabarty developed an oil-eating bacterium that could be used to clean up oil spills. He filed patents on the process of using the bacteria in such clean-up efforts, but he also filed a patent on the bacteria itself. His patent application on the bacteria was rejected because under the 'products of nature' doctrine, US patent law did not allow for patents over living organisms. Chakrabarty appealed the US Patent and Trade Office (USPTO) decision and ultimately the US Supreme Court agreed with him and extended patent protection to his genetically engineered microorganism, in part because while the entity was living it was not a product of nature but rather the product of a laboratory. Thus ended, or rather complicated, the products of nature doctrine.

The products of nature doctrine has long been part of established US Supreme Court patent law (Conley 2009, 112), as has the invention/discovery distinction in most countries. As Conley puts it, 'Although its precise theoretical roots are somewhat murky and still debated, the fundamental point is that the mere discovery of a naturally occurring phenomenon is not patentable because it is not an invention' (2009, 113). *Chakrabarty* was among the first cases to distinguish between a living organism as found in nature and one that was created in the lab.

In cases dealing with the products of nature doctrine, the court has used the labour of the scientist to help distinguish between the naturally occurring object and the product of a laboratory process. For example, in the case of John Moore, where the University of California used Moore's spleen to create a lucrative cancer-fighting agent, the court found that while the doctors had violated their fiduciary duty by failing to inform Moore of the nature of his ongoing treatment (which was for their research purposes), they also found that Moore had no proprietary right in the product of their research because the work done in the laboratory had taken a product of nature (his spleen) and remastered it into a scientific product that could be patented without his consent (Halbert 2005). The raw material of the spleen as found in Moore's body was not patentable as a product of nature, but the resulting product derived from his spleen could be patented.

The distinction remains intact even in the aftermath of the highly publicized 2013 *Myriad Genetics* case heard by the US Supreme Court. In the Myriad case, the Court determined that naturally occurring DNA could not be the subject of a patent, but that cDNA, which is the product of laboratory work, can be patented (Barraclough 2013). The key distinction was that the BCRA1 and BCRA2 genes had been discovered not invented, while the cDNA was indeed an invention (Leong 2014, 677). While many see the Myriad case as a victory for those fighting against the patenting of life, the ultimate implication of the Myriad decision is far more complex, and at least in the initial aftermath, there remains uncertainty about what the full implications will be. A product derived from nature, even if it is DNA, can still be patented after the Myriad decision, if the derived genetic organism, or gene sequence, is not one that existed before in nature. Furthermore, at the international level, Australia, Japan, and the EU allow for gene patents if there is evidence of usefulness (Barraclough 2013), and so there is no international standard as of yet. Thus, while the 2013 US Myriad case was significant, it did not eliminate the possibility of patenting genes or synthesized versions of them. As Leong puts it, there is still no bright line for how much human invention is necessary to meet patentability standards around the world (2014, 678). As such, and given the advance of technical capacity, scope for what is becoming available for patent application at least is radically expanding. Patents over genes are just one example of this political economy. In the next section, we will investigate the issue of seed patents and the effort to assert a farmer's right over the seed owner's rights.

SEED PATENTS AND RESISTANCE

For most of the history of agriculture, farmers cultivated crops using seeds that could be stored from year to year, shared or bought, and – once acquired – became the property of the farmer to use as s/he saw fit. Countries would house seed banks to preserve the biodiversity of seed crops, and from these public resources, farmers were able to introduce new seeds into their crop rotations.

Using the same logic as was highlighted above in the patenting of genes, however, agricultural corporations have been privatizing seeds and developing the legal infrastructure to marginalize farmers and shift the power of agricultural production to the owners of the seed as a patented subject matter. This history tracks back through the whole 20th century, but has intensified with the advent of TRIPS.

As multinational agribusiness has come to dominate agricultural production, a different approach to seed breeding and exchange has emerged. While always the subject of property rights, the insertion of IP into the seed business has fundamentally changed the balance of rights between the farmer and the seed breeder. Where prior to the insertion of IP into the seed, a seed was sold to the farmer at which point the farmer could then use the seed in any manner that met his or her interests, today's seeds come with restrictive licensing agreements and the ongoing control over the seed by the major agribusinesses. Thus, today's farmer may have a license to plant the seeds s/he has purchased, but the license does not extend to saving the remaining seeds to plant the next year or giving or sharing these seeds with a neighbour. The license prohibits farmers from breeding new plants and of creating new hybrids. The license does allow the company from which s/he purchased the seed to inspect both his/her crops and the crops of his/her neighbours to ensure that the seeds were being used properly (Monsanto 2014). Where once IP resided in the tangible expression/formula or blueprint for a workable invention, not the individual physical object (book, car or pill), today IP in the seed itself (just as in an iTune or e-book) blurs the distinction between intellectual and physical property rights and extends ownership over the objects themselves, just as blurring the idea/expression and discovery/intention distinctions has extended IP in similar ways.

The innovative overreach of IP law is the legal ability to continue to own the seed after its sale. Monsanto owns the patent on what is called sterile seed technology, termed the 'terminator gene' by activists (Charles 2012). The technology makes it possible for its patent owner, Monsanto, to produce a sterile seed that terminates at the end of a growing cycle if it is not used. While Monsanto (2015) has promised (since 1999) not to deploy this technology, the creation of sterile seed technology gives agricultural corporations a method for controlling access to food and what can be grown. The promise not to deploy remains theirs to keep or to go back on. Reengineering seed in this manner, building IP control into nature itself (owning the world *through* ideas), is an attempt to maximize the profit of seed corporations, who of course derived their original seed stock from the collective shared seed knowledge of the planet. Such practices were not designed for the betterment of humanity as such.

International regulations and technical mechanisms governing the use of seeds are designed to benefit the seed owner and not the farmer. There are now sui generis IPRs under the International Union for the Protection of New Varieties of Plants (UPOV), an agency created when the International Convention for the Protection of New Varieties of Plants was adopted in 1961, and the powers accorded this convention have been radically increased with the advent of WTO/TRIPS. UPOV is an agreement that limits the ability of farmers to save and share seeds but which supports the 'rights' of multinational seed corporations to control their plant varieties globally. Through patents on seeds themselves, the farmer has been disenfranchised from the centuries-old practice of seed saving (Oguamanam 2014, 241–242). Seeking to prevent nature itself from making unauthorized copies (in the form of fertile seeds) would place that which defined life in the first place under corporate control.

Patents and associated licensing agreements are of growing importance for the protection of genetically modified organisms (GMOs) and the broader agri-industrial business model. To secure rights over seeds and further dis-enfranchise farmers, corporations such as Monsanto have initiated litigation against farmers whose fields have been contaminated by their proprietary seeds. In 2013, the US Supreme Court sided with Monsanto against a collection of organic farmers and the Organic Seed Growers and Trade Association in their efforts to try to defend themselves against Monsanto's aggressive practice of suing farmers whose fields have been contaminated by Monsanto's GM seeds (Hauck 2014). Farmers throughout the global south have sought to resist these global seed practices, but the law remains stacked against the farmer.

We can only begin to sketch the global implications of patenting seeds as well as the privatization and transfer of knowledge that is the result. Chidi Oguamanam sums up the issue as such:

> Beyond marginalization of the public sphere, IP overreach implements a neo-liberal agenda that evaluates innovation through the prisms of capitalist inter-ests and formal scientific rules. That approach alienates and, often, excludes alternative knowledge production efforts, which reflect fairness and openness in the production and distribution of knowledge. (2014, 238)

Interestingly, many corporations, including those asserting proprietary rights over seeds, claim to be working for the betterment of humanity as a whole. The claim being made is that a monopoly over future foods will create the profit incentives necessary to finance and create new and more efficient/ resilient plants and animals to meet future food needs. Such claims have worked their way back into the primary national and international patent agencies as a justification for the importance of the patent system. Yet, as the terminator seed example illustrates, such a corporate approach to food puts the protection of profits before human need. As such, building future food security on a foundation of corporate monopoly control raises very serious dangers. Can private monopolies be trusted with such power over the basic essentials of human life? In the final sections of this chapter, we chart efforts to demonstrate the benefits of the patent system for human health and development and the efforts being made to ensure that innovative technologies are best used. It is certainly not the case that private profit, secured by legal monopolies, ensures by itself any such outcome.

ACCESS TO MEDICINE

Despite decades of advocacy for better access to medication, especially access to life-saving treatment for diseases such as HIV/AIDS, the global patent system and the regulatory regime that exists to protect the rights of patent holders continues to play a significant role in limiting access to medicine on the basis of ability or inability to pay monopoly-inflated prices. The issue of access to medicine made international news in the late 1990s and early 2000s when South Africa was sued by the pharmaceutical industry for attempting to deal with the public health crisis brought on by the spread of HIV/AIDS. In response to the spread of HIV/AIDS, South Africa sought to provide affordable access to generic versions of patented HIV/AIDS medications, a move that was resisted by the industry as a violation of their IPRs. Advocacy groups like the Treatment Action Campaign were able to focus international criticism on the industry for placing patents and profits above the lives of people (Halbert 2005; Halbert and May 2005). The global outcry that emerged in relation to the access to medicine issue ushered in what Daniel Gervais calls the 'second phase' of TRIPS. In other words, the controversy over access to HIV/AIDS medication initiated a backlash against the 'maximalist' (or 'strong') extension and protection of IP set out in the original TRIPS agreement. A 'minimalist' (or 'flexible') approach to IP protection is championed by those interested in better access to medicine among other things (Gervais 2014, 101–102). In the ensuing years, access to medicine has become one of the central issues emblematic of the systematic problems with a patent system that privileges private patent monopolies over human life.

After almost two decades of efforts to shape the global debate on access to medicine around issues of health care as a human right and policies that would make the creation and distribution of generic drugs easier, the pharmaceutical industry continues to lobby for tougher laws and for even more expansive protection. Activists engaged in the ongoing struggle to define the issue of access to medicine in terms of people over profits have sought to publicize the power patent holders exert over the global political economy. South Africa as a developing economy remains an important example of how patents shape social justice issues from the local to the global. In 2014, South Africa was still attempting to revise its patent law to align with section 27 of the state constitution that requires access to medicine as a human right. Such a move is strongly opposed by the pharmaceutical industry that hired lobbyists and lawyers to derail the effort (Darch 2014b, 640). From the patent perspective, access to medicine must always come at the price established by the patent owner.

While the issue of HIV/AIDS sparked global attention about access to medicine, the interplay of patents and access to medicine goes well beyond this suite of drugs. Big Pharma (the multinational corporations constituting the primary patent-based pharmaceutical industry) use patents to control access to drugs across all fields of endeavour. One of the reasons why there is such global controversy over the production of generic drugs is that pharmaceutical companies controlling the patents seek to keep monopoly prices on drugs for as long as possible (Spruill and Cunningham 2005). It is well known that once a drug leaves the protection of its patents, the prices fall significantly.

Generic drug producers in India, Brazil and Thailand, however, have all sought to resist the global imposition of patents on their production of many life-saving drugs, arguing instead that domestic laws provide for the manufacture of generics when public health is at issue. Brazil, for example, has been especially proactive in preserving the ability to manufacture affordable generic versions of life-saving drugs. The Brazilian government is keen to protect its generic drug industry and has continued to resist the global pharmaceutical industry lobby's efforts to force them to play by the patent rules established to ensure monopoly profits for Big Pharma (Wharton School 2006). While the production of generic drugs in Brazil has diminished the profit margins of patent owners, it has enhanced the affordability of drugs for Brazilians. Additionally, Brazil has been able to control HIV infection rates by ensuring people have better access to the appropriate medication and they have done so in direct opposition to the wishes of global pharmaceutical corporations.

The use of patents to protect pharmaceutical products should be a deeply controversial issue. Developed states on behalf of the pharmaceutical industry attempt to halt the distribution of generic drugs produced and sold for a fraction of the cost of those remaining under patent protection. India, Thailand and Brazil have been resisting an attempt by the developed world to collapse the distinction between 'fake' drugs and 'counterfeit' drugs. For these countries 'fake' drugs are those without active ingredients that are sold – falsely – as real medicinal drugs by means of false packaging, most often copying the packaging of the patent holder's 'real' product. False packaging that imitates an established brand or trademark is – legally speaking – counterfeiting (trademark issues will be discussed in more detail in the next chapter). Passing pills off as containing a certain chemical composition when this is untrue is fraud. As such, 'fake' drugs involve both counterfeiting and fraud. Generic drugs, on the other hand, do contain the same active ingredients as the patent holder's original – and that is why they infringe the patent. A generic drug is simply the 'real' drug made by someone other than the original patent holder. It would be perfectly possible for a particularly hardened – and highly skilled – criminal to go to the trouble of actually making a real (chemically speaking) version of a particular medication and then to package it falsely to increase its price, thereby breaching patent and trademark, even while not committing fraud. Nonetheless this is very unlikely. On the other hand, government-sanctioned generic drugs are not falsely packaged. They challenge patent holder control, but they do not commit either fraud or counterfeiting. However, patent holding western pharmaceutical lobbies are now seeking to have the term 'counterfeit' drugs used to describe 'generic' drugs. For these countries of the global south, what negotiators for developed states and the drug lobbyists associated with these states are seeking to call counterfeit drugs are the generic drugs that make access to real medication affordable. Attempting to blur the line between generic drugs that are neither fraudulent nor counterfeit, but which do infringe patents, and 'fake' drugs that are fraudulent in content and/or counterfeit in packaging is a deliberate effort to undermine developing country drug industries and to consolidate profits for Big Pharma (Sen 2012). It is of course possible that real, efficacious generic medicines, if acquired by criminals, could be repackaged in counterfeit (trademark-infringing) form for sale at a higher price, but if safe and effective generics were available, this market in counterfeits would itself be undercut. That patent holders worry more about loss of control than they do about access to medicine by those who cannot afford monopoly prices speaks volumes. That developing countries have continued to resist such moral panics which seek to blur the distinction between generics and counterfeits and have upheld their own right to produce generic drugs to meet substantive health needs in the global south manifests what Gervais calls the recalibration phase of IP formation discussed in Chapter 2.

While industry players perpetuate a narrative of high-risk research that justifies monopoly protection of the resultant products, such a story, while good public relations, does not capture the complexity of how drugs are researched and developed. It does, however, supply pharmaceutical companies with a justification for strong patent protection, emphasizing their own contributions to the process relative to the contributions made by government-funded research, non-profit sponsored research and, of course, the non-commercial research completed by academics that may not always directly translate into practical commodities but which often underpins later commercial products.

AZT is an excellent example of such appropriative practices. A 1999 Health Action International report found that AZT was initially invented by the US National Cancer Institute in the 1960s and its first use as an antiretroviral was in 1984 by the National Cancer Institute (Schulte-Hillen 1999). Despite its origins and the help of public funding, a patent was issued to Burroughs Wellcome for the use of AZT for AIDS treatment in part because by the mid-1980s it was an orphan drug (Schulte-Hillen 1999). Note the contrast here between orphan copyright works that IP claimants may return to if that work is later used by others (as discussed in Chapter 3) and these research findings from non-commercial actors that appear open to repatenting when a profit seems possible, even when their orphan status might have expected them to have fallen into the public domain. Patentability, however, rendered the treatment too expensive for most in the developing world. While only a brief example, AZT highlights how pharmaceutical company justifications for strong patent monopolies, the insinuation that absolute control in their hands is warranted as return and incentive for their singular efforts, is deeply misleading and hides a far more complex landscape of research and development where industry privatizes the public work of other actors.

TECHNOLOGY TRANSFER

The relationship between IP and economic development has been central to both justifications of expanding IP protection and critiques of IP. The use of IP to further economic development through technology transfer to the global south is one of the underlying justifications for the incorporation of WIPO as a UN specialized agency (Halbert 2007). However, the ability of an international IP regime to promote development through foreign direct investment (FDI) and technology transfer is much more complex and contradictory than WIPO suggests. Gervais summarizes many of these complexities and suggests that IP as a developmental tool has not been shown decisively to 'produce net developmental benefits' (2014, 102). First, the size of the markets might influence a company's interest in investing regardless of the level of IP protection (think about China versus any small least developed country). Second, the perception of IP protection in a given industry may have more impact than any reality of protection. Third, countries with domestic adaptive R&D sectors will encourage more investment than countries without (Gervais 2014, 102). In other words, technology transfer and FDI is not a given in an IP-rich world, even as it is used as a justification for global expansion and enforcement.

Matthew Rimmer's research on patent's relationship to environmentally harmful and potentially friendlier technologies also brings into question the claim that patents are a panacea for global development. Given the fact that many industries utilizing patents do so to protect products and inventions that are environmentally detrimental, the patent system itself plays a role in our modern ecological crisis (Rimmer 2011, 2014). Enforcing patents on old technologies may reward their retention only if enforcing patents on newer more environmentally friendly technologies makes their adoption prohibitively expensive, especially in poorer countries. Attempts to encourage technology transfer – such that poorer countries might adopt clean technologies – have therefore been inhibited by strong patent protection, and efforts to limit patent enforcement to enable faster take-up in the global south have been firmly rebuffed by patent holding lobbies. As Rimmer points out, recent international negotiations to deal with climate change have not resulted in any meaning-ful method of transferring clean patented technologies globally (2014, 729). Countries throughout the global south advocate for solutions to climate change that would be made possible through affordable access to patented technologies. However, such mechanisms have stalled in the face of signifi-cant resistance on the part of patent holders (Rimmer 2014). Given the serious implications of a failure to address climate change and its associated energy-related problems, if patents hinder technology transfer more than they help it, this brings their legitimacy into question.

PATENTS FOR HUMANITY?

Given the criticisms of the patent system and of IP generally that are now part of the global debate over the value of such regimes, both WIPO and USPTO have initiated programmes designed to demonstrate the value of patents and the contributions the patent system makes to the world. The USPTO has cre-ated a 'patents for humanity' prize to promote the view that patentable subject matter is being used to contribute to the social good. In 2013, awards were given in areas ranging from health and medicine to agriculture and environ-mentally clean technologies. The award recipients read like a global corporate Who's Who, with companies such as DuPont, Proctor and Gamble and Micro-soft receiving awards for their technologies. While there is no doubt that many of these innovations may do good work globally, such a prize can be seen as a form of greenwashing of corporate practices, given the overall reluctance shown by such actors to sacrifice any profit in order to achieve wider environmental and/or developmental improvement through affordable technology transfer. Rimmer documents how corporate lobbies have systematically and successfully removed any discussion/questioning of IPRs from environmental and developmental treaty negotiations, having all such discussions referred to IP-specific forums, which they have successfully controlled or at least contained. As such, within negotiations over environment and development issues, IP is only ever referred to as a 'neutral' and 'positive' vehicle for incentivizing innovation. If IP rewards innovation, it must be protected. Any question concerning affordable distribution is externalized as something for consumers, states and NGOs (not corporations) to pay for. While this defence of private interests is understandable, it does show that, left to itself, private business cannot be expected to act for the common good. As Rimmer (2012) concludes in his analysis of the USPTO's 'patents for humanity' programme regarding ongoing access to medicine, the programme might provide some minor incentives to participants to more equitably distribute their commercial products, at least while under public scrutiny, but does little to encourage or provide access to medicine more broadly. In essence the awards extended to winners of the 'patents for humanity' prize are not evidence of the value of patents per se, in enabling access, but rather a means of tempering, or at least appearing to temper, patents' major weakness – that they make knowledge available only at the holder's discretion, usually for payment at monopoly prices.

'Patents for humanity' does provide a window through which to explore aspects of the global economy within which such patents flow. For example, Procter and Gamble (P&G) won the 2013 award for clean technology for their patented water purification technology. P&G developed a powder that can be used to purify water and remove virtually all pathogens as well as coagulate and remove dirt from drinking water. It is thus a vital product that could be of enormous benefit given the fact that the vast majority of the world's population have no access to clean drinking water. P&G created this technology in collaboration with the Centers for Disease Control and Prevention (CDC) and it is now distributed by NGOs throughout the world. According to P&G, over 7 billion litres of clean drinking water have now been provided by distributing this easy-to-use purification technology to the global south ('Children's Safe Drinking Water Impact' 2014). While P&G initially invested in the technology as a for-profit venture, its failure to generate a profit meant P&G shifted focus and began selling the product at cost to humanitarian organizations (Baddache 2008, 2).

Despite its failure as a significant profit generator, P&G continues to control, produce and sell the product and has established the 'Children's Safe Drinking Water Program' to brand the product as part of its corporate responsibility efforts (we will cover issues of branding in Chapter 5). Individuals interested in supporting the program can either purchase the packets to donate themselves or make a donation to P&G directly so that they can distribute the powder to targeted areas. Thus, while the product may not make a taxable profit, it does still cover its costs, and it brings additional benefits to P&G in the form of positive corporate relations. If P&G sells 'at cost', the program is thereby paid for by donations and NGO purchases of the technology. The $35m figure, P&G notes in their website, as having been donated to the project mainly represents the cost of developing the product in the first place. Yet, there is no mention here regarding how the state-funded CDC was involved in the program or of how their support helped fund the original research into the product. As such:

1. Innovation that combined state and commercial organizations is now privately 'patented' and kept the monopoly property of commercial actors.
2. The patent holder still retains control over production 'at cost' (set by them), rather than being made available for all to produce and distribute more widely.
3. To date only one litre of clean water per human being on earth has been made available by means of this patent's regulating/distributing of technology.

This supposed 'triumph' of patents for human needs is at best rather weak and might in fact be seen as rather a shocking triumph of control over human need. As an example of how patents might work to expand access to essential and life-saving technologies (water purification in this case), it simply reflects the underlying problems of the patent system itself. The study of access to medicine, technology transfer, agribusiness and biotechnology suggests that the ownership of innovation, especially concentrated as it is into multinational corporate hands, is part of the problem to be solved, not the solution itself.

CONCLUSION

Patents, like copyrights, exist to protect a global flow of products within a private property and profit-based economy. We now live in a world where access to food, medicine, clean drinking water and much more is regulated by patents. While patents only last for a limited time, the patent thickets that grow around any given technology mean that a product's entry into the public domain may not be that simple. Rather, corporations increasingly wrap products and processes in layers of IP (from patents to trademarks, to copyrights) and increasingly sell licenses to access products for specific times and uses, rather than selling products as such. In this way, ownership over ideas, expressions, technologies and brands can be concentrated and regulatory structures can be put in place to ensure ownership remains virtually perpetual, even after a product is ostensibly sold. The system itself may produce social benefits, or it may not. When such benefits arise, they are slow in coming for the less well-off and always secondary to the central purpose of patents and IP generally to ensure a monopoly and thus to maximize profit for the patent holder. When lack of access leads to social harm, the primacy of IP protection is once again brought forward as a necessary evil of pecuniary incentive, against which the suffering of the poor is then but the lesser, but equally necessary, evil.

In response to the patenting trends discussed here, there is a growing global resistance to the logic of privatizing life. What we are witnessing are two competing narratives of how we ought to organize the world. The divide between these approaches has to do with choices about how far one thinks the commodification that is at the heart of the patent process ought to go. For those resisting patents on genetic material and other living things, and those advocating for affordable access to medical and environmental innovations for all, human life and access to affordable innovations are considered more important values than market considerations and profit margins. However, the framing of patents today asserts that only through commodification of such knowledge do people find the incentive to invent. While any given scientist may innovate and be driven by intellectual pursuits, and much research takes place in and through publically funded or charitable agencies, the biotech-nology industry with its patent portfolios seeks to obscure such motives for and sources of innovation, in its attempt to claim the right to own lucrative products. From this vantage point, it is merely a happy accident if research and development provides life-saving technologies. Thus, from the logic of the industry, payment for access to their property is required and if you cannot pay, then sadly, you cannot have access.

The ethical issues that emerge when such access is denied are serious concerns for all. There is a big difference between denying someone a life-saving treatment by pricing a medicine so high as to make it unaffordable and refusing someone access to a luxury good. Likewise, failure to distribute envi-ronmentally friendly technology will impact humanity more seriously than the failure to distribute the latest music or computer game. Patent holders do not deny that there are real and serious problems that need solutions. Rather they deny that the social dimension of these problems (the issue of access and equity) is their problem. Patent holders, rather, present themselves as merely providers of technical solutions that need to be paid. Patent holders claim it is for users, charities (including their own corporate social responsibility depart-ments), citizens and states to provide such payment, though they are keen to retain the power to determine the price such payment should be. Technical detachment, the claim that patents merely deliver technical solutions through morally neutral – financial – incentives, makes the 'problem' of distribution just another 'externality', not the proper business of private business. This representation of moral neutrality and technical efficiency is multiply misleading.

Advocates for strong patent protection argue that it is the monopoly rights guaranteed by patents that make innovation possible. However, on closer inspection, as innovation in the pharmaceutical sector demonstrates, public funding, charitable efforts and university research are all essential to the process of invention. Private incentive is simply not the sole source of innovation. Privatizing the end results as the creation of a single corporation misrepresents the reality of research and development. Protecting such innovations as if they were the simple results of private endeavour also leads to socially damaging consequences. In all the areas discussed in this chapter, from the struggle for affordable medicine, over issues of access to environmentally sustainable technologies, through claims made as to the best means of incentivizing and distributing innovation itself, and efforts by IP advocates to present patents as supportive in distributing life-saving technologies, the core tensions of contemporary IP law are evident: between shared knowledge and private ownership over ideas, between progress in knowledge alone and progress in terms of human need, and between general development and a global harmonization around one particular set of dominant interests.

5

TRADEMARK, DESIGNS AND IDENTIFIERS IN QUESTION

Global network capitalism's outsourcing of the production of luxury goods separates production and composition of a product from the trademarks such objects carry. The trademark as embodied by the brand seeks to associate a positive image with the product and to detach the brand from any moral or legal implications related to its production such as the exploitation of sweatshop labour and environmental harm. Detachment of production from symbolic mark and meaning, as well as from action and moral consequence, is mirrored in the pirate capitalism of counterfeiters and the reflexive consumption of 'fakes'. In both cases the brand ('authentic' or fake) obscures the conditions of production (*alienation*) and encourages uncritical consumption based upon the image of the product, not the product itself (*commodity fetishism*). Global networks of production help to detach action from moral consequences or the consideration of such moral consequences (either in the legal or non-legal forms of free-market deregulation). Global networks can also be used to highlight otherwise invisible victims of just such amoral forms of deregulation, including those working in sweatshops or otherwise exploited in the production of global goods. In the context of trademark protection and piracy, TNCs claim to be the victims of massive global counterfeiting, but also stand accused of being the villains in such distributed networks.

Marks indicating geographical origin present similar patterns of paradox and contradiction. Protecting particular places through global legal frames can add value to locally produced goods, but those locals best able to take advantage of the resulting market opportunity are those already linked into global flows of resources, knowledge and influence. Just as locality is a contested construction, not a natural and organic unity, so global network capitalism is a negotiated and contested assemblage – as disputes discussed below between economic elites and dominant states over protection for designs demonstrate.

In what follows we first examine the meaning of trademark and counterfeiting. We then examine the rise of what Chon (2014) calls 'cognitive capitalism', where struggles to control the signalling strength of trademarks comes to the fore. We then address the relationship between trademarks and (a) global network capitalism in its transnational 'outsourced' form and (b) global network capitalism in its transgressive 'outlawed' form (counterfeit capitalism). The tension between protecting property and freeing markets in global network capitalism is highlighted. Then, we explore GIs. Akin in part to trademarks, GIs prevent the very forms of outsourcing that have come to dominate the production of goods linked to trademarks, yet both GIs and trademarks seek monopoly controls, just on different grounds (historical location rather than geographically detached association). The contradictions already drawn out in the chapter – between demands for monopoly control to protect property rights and for free trade that deregulates rights of various kinds – are then further illustrated in relation to design law where states still diverge on the balance between protecting creation and avoiding protectionism.

TRADEMARKS VERSUS COUNTERFEITS

The 1994 Agreement on TRIPS defines a trademark as any 'sign, or combination of signs, capable of distinguishing the goods or services of one undertaking from those of other undertakings' (cited in Chon 2014, 171). Such marks usually require national registration, but are increasingly recognized internationally (from Berne to TRIPS and beyond). Through reregistration trademarks have unlimited duration. Trademarks identify the maker, not the content of the thing made. Regulative marks – such as marks developed by third parties to indicate fair trade practices, organic status, safety standards, etc. – are different, but trademark holders may seek to link with such standards to enhance the value of their brand in the minds of consumers.

Brand associations may link trademarks with respected regulative principles, or with less defined cultural norms and values (Lury 2004; Klein 2009). Brand and brand association link with marks but are not themselves the IP that is legally protected. For example, the Nike swoosh is a mark, as is their phrase 'just do it', but the brand itself is the general relationship between the protected trademarks, of which there are many, and a larger consumer recognition of particular associations linked to the mark. This wider recognition is what some call the 'social imaginary' (see below) built up by branding around a mark. Each mark is individually registered and thus is legally protected as IP. The wider brand that is built upon the multiplicity of trademarks does not enjoy legal protection but is more abstract. A mark with positive brand identification commands a higher price and is thereby as attractive to rights holders as to 'pirates'. Infringement of trademarked goods is called counterfeiting.

TRIPS sets out that: '"Counterfeit trademark goods" shall mean any goods, including packaging, bearing, without authorization, a trademark that is identical to that trademark validly registered in respect of such goods that cannot be distinguished in its essential aspects from such a trademark' (cited in Rojek 2014, 192). Stretching global supply networks increases the value of marks (as they can be sold everywhere), but bigger markets also increase the motive and potential to counterfeit them. Furthermore, once production is globally outsourced, unauthorized counterfeit branded products can also be sold worldwide, often being manufactured in the same outsourced factories and distributed via the same outsourced delivery networks, as are used by brand holders to cut costs. If the trademarked product is made in an outsourced and offshore location, it is far harder for regulative standards to be upheld, and in many cases they simply are not. Thus, global supply networks stretch – perhaps to a breaking point – the link between regulative marks and trademarks and, as such, further weaken the inhibitors that exist to purchasing counterfeits.

Brand citizenship (Chon 2014) is an evolving effort to try to get high-profile brands to develop good trade practices associated with the production of their products. Those developing the concept of brand citizenship want to hold trademark owners accountable for the labour practices of distant and outsourced suppliers and thereby raise worker and production standards across the globe. Brand pirates, on the other hand, undermine monopoly prices, making 'luxury' goods more affordable, even while challenging the notion of 'authenticity' in such goods (see discussion below). The contradictions of contemporary global network capitalism, tensions between inclusion and exclusion, markets and monopoly protection, and between harmonized ethical regulation and liberal deregulation are neatly captured in this contrast. Brand citizenship seeks to promote ethical outcomes through the channels of IP enforcement, while counterfeit capitalism increases access (through lower prices) by the suspension of such controls.

GLOBAL SUPPLY NETWORKS, SIGNS AND SIGNALS

Global network capitalism has spread production and distribution across the globe, even while seeking legal control over these global processes. The old term 'supply chain' suggests too linear a relationship. 'Global supply networks' captures things better (Chon 2014, 172). Where chains imply strong links, networks point to the multiplicity of connections. A buyer can now drive down prices through playing multiple outsourced suppliers against one another, but, at the same time, such outsourced suppliers are now better able to feed counterfeits up into the marketplace through multiple modes of (lawful and unlawful) distribution. Such networks will be more clearly elaborated below.

Copyrighted goods are more purely informational and so can circulate freely online. Patent-rich items require more physical embodiment than most people can produce for themselves, at least before 3D printing becomes ubiquitous. Downloading a song, for example, is easier than applying a patented formula to manufacture medicine. Because of the infrastructure involved, patent-rich items require production arrangements that temper even the enthusiasm of transnational firms from outsourcing everything to developing countries (Crouch 2004). Trademarks sit somewhere in between the digital flow of copyrighted goods and patent infringement, which requires manufacturing facilities. Copying a drug formula is far harder than counterfeiting the packaging of that drug. A generic drug may infringe the patent holder's rights, as it is still the same chemical formula, and hence requires the ability to manufacture it. Appropriating the trademarked packaging of that drug to sell fake pills in counterfeit packaging is much less labour- and cost-intensive. While governments in some developing countries have legislated for the suspension of patents relating to urgently needed medicines, which then allows for generics to be produced, criminals will be more attracted to trademark-infringing counterfeiting. Adding 'fake'/'knock off' labelling to manufactured objects (handbags, clothing, perfumes, etc.) can be done more easily anywhere in the world than would be the case, for example, in making patent-rich semiconductors, computers, medicines and aeroplane parts.

Coordinating production in low-cost parts of the world and sale in wealthier markets is made possible via digital communication. Global outsourcing of production means the mark (and associated branding) becomes a rights holder's 'bridge' between production and consumption of a product, the central node holding their network together. Defending exclusivity in using such marks/brand identifiers is, therefore, more important for trademark holders than is their need to retain direct product quality control over individual suppliers. Trademark defends the right to use certain signs commonly identified with particular companies. Specific expressions and innovations would be protected by copyright and patent respectively.

What trademark protects – in so far as the mark protects anything at all – is a signal. Marks are assumed to signal something to consumers that they are willing to pay 'extra' for relative to a parallel product not sending that signal. Counterfeiters seek to render the network fully distributed by bypassing mark-controlling bridges, appropriating the signal of the mark and thus diverting potential profits towards their business enterprises and away from the owner of the mark. Undoing blockages in this way also leads to reduced prices, which then bind consumers into a mainly knowing collusion within a counterfeit culture (Rojek 2014).

THE INVISIBLE VICTIMS OF COGNITIVE CAPITALISM

Margaret Chon (2014) refers to the emergence of a new 'cognitive capitalism'. Expanding media and increasingly interactive media creates new spaces in which demand is created and preferences negotiated and performed. 'Cognitive capitalism' extends older techniques of marketing and advertising in the attempt to mine minds and to thereby better anticipate and manipulate preferences. Trademarks become part of an interactive media signalling process branding seeks to manage.

What is it then that trademarks signal? There is a significant difference between what the law actually says a mark signals and what a brand linked to a mark may seek to claim is being signalled (Chon 2014). Trademark's function in law is to prohibit 'passing off' products of one company as the products of another company, but marks have come (in error) to be associated with claims regarding the trustworthiness of the product itself. 'Tarnishment' refers to when a company dilutes the reputation of another company's trademark by using that trademark in relation to inferior products or products unrelated to the mark holder's actual portfolio of products. This may reduce trust in the lawful trademark holder. However, if the lawful trademark holder were to attach their mark to lower quality or tangential goods, this in no way infringes trademark law. If consumers find out, they may withdraw their trust. Brand management is designed to avoid this. This may involve maintaining standards or by obscuring or outsourcing lower standards.

Trademark law does not protect customers from mark holders. Marks only protect mark holders from non-holders. If you trust company X to pay living wages and use organic materials, you will want to know you are buying products from company X, not counterfeit products from company Y, trading on the reputation of company X's commitments but not paying the extra costs involved. However, while trademark law protects company X from company Y's infringement of its name, trademark in no way addresses the question of whether company X really is 'trustworthy' in the first place. Many paper-making companies, for example, want to be known for sustainable practices, but still get their pulp from old growth forests, even if by outsourced routes, which allow them to claim ignorance and avoid responsibility. This might be dishonest, but as long as the dishonesty is that of the legal trademark holder, it is not a breach of IP. Just because company Y wants to cash in on company X's reputation does not mean that company X's reputation is deserved. If brand X really does not improve your social standing, attractiveness or sporting ability, or if its 'social imaginary' (the association created in its promotion) turns out to be false, this is in no way a matter of trademark law – though it may constitute false advertising.

Trademark protects its holder's name from misappropriation. It does not protect either consumers or producers from such rights holders. It may, in fact, rather increase the scope for further deception and/or exploitation. For example, outsourcing and offshoring of production reduces the visibility, oversight and responsibility a company holds over its labour practices, environmental regulations, health and safety codes, etc. Trademarks, brands and labels are more easily detached from the taint of sweatshop labour and environmentally destructive practices once production is distributed and detached. Global network capitalist processes of detachment and distribution make it necessary for transnational firms to enforce the symbolic and legal link (through the mark) between production by others and their ownership of the product. Yet, detachment and distribution delink symbolic meaning and legal liability, products and their production.

Margaret Chon (2014) and others (Seidman 2007; Miller and Williams 2009; Cline 2012) highlight the invisible victims of outsourcing and how an inappropriate trust in the signalling function of trademarks may in fact increase that invisibility. Trademark holders want positive reputations. Legally, trademarks do not regulate the truth claims of trademark holders. However, exposure of poor conditions in outsourced factories can cause lawful rights holders reputational harm. To this extent, Chon advocates 'brand citizenship' as a counterforce to the one-dimensional use of trademarks within 'cognitive capitalism'. Global networks afford scope to circulate evidence regarding the consequences of outsourcing and hence enable communication between producers and consumers that bypasses corporate communications. Brand citizenship seeks to hold corporations to account. While seeking to work with trademark holders' desire to maintain their reputations, Chon is not suggesting 'brand citizenship' can render reputation management sufficient to reform global network capitalism's propensity to deregulate wages and conditions even as it seeks to further regulate the control of IP. Global outsourcing has been used to bypass regulatory measures and marks of safety, pay and quality. Brand citizenship can point the finger. Alone, it is not enough.

TRUST IN SIGNS?

Chris Rojek (2014) identifies a further contradiction in the logic of informational capitalism. Edward Bruner (1994) distinguishes 'aura', 'verisimilitude' and 'authorization' in what makes an 'authentic reproduction'. Aura denotes a near-perfect approximation of the original; verisimilitude a near-enough approximation. Something that carries 'authorization' carries some sign of 'certification' irrespective of its origins or composition. The sign of certification is, in this case, the mark of authenticity irrespective of the marked object's actual origins or composition. Reflexive consumers (of luxury goods at least) operate just like trademark holders. Some consumers may be deceived. This possibility is particularly acute in relation to counterfeit medication and technical products where false labelling may deceive purchasers as to the substantive content. The reflexive consumer of style goods knowingly buys the mark itself, not the object's physical qualities and origins, at the lowest price. The mark signals on this consumer's behalf. The 'fake' mark does not signal origin or quality to the consumer any more than a 'real' mark, legally speaking, guarantees physical origin or quality of composition. The consumer is sending the message with the mark. Real or fake it is not telling them anything.

Following Bruner, after a fashion, trademark holding transnational firms outsource 'aura' and 'verisimilitude' to others, retaining only the 'authorization' function of marking certification. Quality, standards and virtue (or their absence) in product and production become detached from the mark. The mark signals the identity of the mark's holder, but it says increasingly little about the product it is attached to. As the mark signals status on behalf of its purchaser with little or no reference to the physical object's qualities, ethics or provenance, so marks perform this same 'empty' function for rights holders.

Trading empty marks may just display reciprocal cynicism, but counterfeit medicines can kill. In the context of IPRs, it is important to keep clear the distinction between generics and counterfeits. Generic pharmaceuticals, for example, are the same chemical compounds as the original but produced without having to license the patents, one of the reasons why they are much cheaper than the patented product. In most cases, generics are legal under domestic laws either because the patent has run out or because the country in question specifically authorizes the production of generics, even in opposition to international conventions that seek to harmonize – i.e. extend – global patent protection (as discussed in Chapter 4). Generic drugs do not use the trademark of the patent holder (if one exists) and so are not 'counterfeits'. Patent-inflated prices combined with poverty – not deception – explain the generics markets in medicines (Millaleo and Cadenas 2014). High profits explain why criminals sell counterfeit medicines (and autoparts, etc.) into lawful supply networks and hence deceive end-users.

A WAR OF ALL AGAINST ALL

Global network capitalism's detachment of production from ownership, and of origin from use/meaning, does not then only occur at the level of the transnational firm seeking to outsource the physical aspects of product and production so that it can concentrate on defending and selling symbolic value added. Additionally, it is mirrored (Rojek rightly argues) in the 'pirate capitalism' of global counterfeiting networks and in the 'pirate cultures' of those willing to purchase such goods. Rojek suggests nihilism follows from simply mirroring global network capitalism's amorality in both counterfeit capitalism and counterfeit culture. Playing the system at its own game may cut prices, but may also cut what vestiges of quality still exist. It takes 'the race to the bottom' already driving legal forms of global network capitalism to new lows. However, if you cannot already afford authorized originals, fakes cannot be worse than what you had before – which was nothing.

Against this vicious circle Chon suggests a virtuous circle, pressing TNCs to live up to the illusion of their own global brand messages, their claims that trademarks denote genuine virtues. Nonetheless, playing the illusions of global network capitalism against themselves (pressing transnational firms to live up to their own misrepresentations) is only a partial immunization of cognitive capitalism against itself. Reputational repair as a reaction to critical brand citizenship assumes the capacity of critics to overcome the kinds of 'information failure' that global network capitalist outsourcing and brand management foster. Building globally networked movements that promote worker and environmental rights is essential for marks to be confronted with the truth beneath their branding. Action must go well beyond simply holding a mirror to TNCs, whether this is in the form of exposing (brand citizenship) or copying (brand piracy) moral detachment and illusions of quality.

HARMONIZATION FOR WHAT AND FOR WHOM?

A trademark should distinguish one producer from another. Does such a capacity for distinction have to be measured? Does recognition somewhere warrant protection everywhere? The US fast food chain McDonald's entry into post-Apartheid South Africa is illustrative (Darch 2014a). During Apartheid, McDonald's did not renew its South African trademark. Could a MacDonald's (spelt differently) trading in South Africa be 'falsely' trading on the US company's name if the US company had no registered trademark there? Others in the country also ran franchises using the name McDonald's. In 1996 a lower court rejected claims for infringement of trademark, dismissing evidence that the US company's name was well known in South Africa because research suggesting this came from an unrepresentative sample of mainly white South Africans. The Supreme Court overturned this verdict. Was it enough that McDonald's was a global corporation for its name to be assumed to be well known everywhere? It appeared so. The global enforcement of a trademark raises the question of 'harmonization' – the doctrine that trademarks (along with other forms of IP) should be judged, extended and upheld equally everywhere. That a name holds a long-standing meaning and association in one place would then become the basis for extending protection over that name and its associated products everywhere. Such global protection creates a near-infinite field of geographically projected claims and counter-claims. As will be seen below in the discussion of GIs, such disputes over priority, scope and extension as much reflect as they address questions of power and injustice when judging who can and cannot own names and the things being named.

GEOGRAPHICAL INDICATIONS

The term 'geographical indication' only entered legal language with the 1994 TRIPS agreement, but draws upon a longer and diverse history of protecting claims to origin and place. Coombe et al. (2014a, 208) note that marks indicating conditions of origin (MICOs) have a longer history. MICOs often link conditions of 'quality, reputation and characteristic' to specific places. For GIs this geographical specificity is key. Within the EU, 'Protected Denomination of Origin' requires a strict linkage of a product's composition to the social and natural characteristics of place. 'Protected Geographical Indication' is less exclusive in that a place name may receive protection even if the product to which the name is associated could be created elsewhere. Coombe et al. (2014a, 208) give the examples of Parmigiano Reggiano cheese and Darjeeling tea as respective cases. In both cases, the products are identified by their region of origin and it is understood that such an association is essential to the success of the product in the global market.

The concept of 'terroir', the binding of place, production and produce, originated in France and is strongly linked to European conceptions of tradition, heritage and patrimony. Coombe et al. (2014a, 208) argue: 'The EU sees GI extension as compensation for the reduction of agricultural subsidies entailed by global trade liberalization'. Using GIs to protect 'traditional' forms of production and product from liberalized free-markets parallels the use of trademark law to protect TNCs against counterfeiting 'free-marketeers' who produce near-identical copies at lower prices because they do not respect the 'authenticity' of the 'original'. The EU and US promote regulation to protect dominant interests just as they will also promote deregulation for the same reasons. When and how such differing strategies are chosen, negotiated and acted upon is therefore complex and not without contradiction. Not only are GIs being sought and applied within the EU itself, but the EU also promotes their adoption and protection in the global south to promote better terms of trade between primary producers and consumers in the north.

Advocates of GIs present: 'representations and assumptions of a singular tradition, deriving from a singular culture, rooted in a singular place, with its own naturally distinctive ecosystem which a "community", holistically imagined, stewards as resources for the future' (Coombe et al. 2014a, 213). This is what Coombe et al. call (after Castoriadis 1987, 1997) the 'social imaginary' of GIs. Such imaginaries are doubly questionable. Holistic, equitable, unified and bounded communities of place neither pre-exist nor do GIs inevitably bring them about. While GIs may promote higher and more equitable returns to primary producers, this is not always true. Such outcomes require overcoming inequalities and exclusions, not simply imagining them away.

Coombe et al. (2014a, 214) cite Moran (1993, 1999) who highlights how France's appellations of origin (some of the earliest and strongest precursors to today's GIs) 'were developed to protect aristocratic traditions and continue to reflect class-based privilege'. Gade's (2004) study of how French appellations are managed to secure elite control over production and profit, exacerbating rather than reducing regional inequalities, is also cited. Such control by 'old' families can be used to exclude immigrants even over many generations. It is hoped, but cannot be guaranteed, that new claimants to GI protection will organize more equitable and inclusive forms of self-governance over how protection is controlled. Mass production, under the label of 'local' produce, may undermine small-scale local producers. Retaining small-scale production leaves producers susceptible to middle men (Chan 2014).

Chan's research in Peru highlights the need for networks of local empowerment to integrate with wider NGOs to overcome both expropriation by bigger producers and marginalization within supply chains. For example, as tequila became a more important global product and as production of mescal increased, an effort was made to standardize production under government regulation. As a result, the Mexican government control over GIs for regional variations on liquors similar to tequila led to mass production and further marginalization of small-scale local producers (Coombe and Aylwin 2009, cited in Coombe et al. 2014a, 217).

A similar story emerges in the global marketing of the South African product trademarked as Rooibos. Colin Darch (2014a, 270–271) points out that the name 'Rooibos' was first registered as a 'trademark' in the US in the 1990s, and this mark was then used to demand royalties from those importing the product from its source – South Africa. This trademark was revoked in 2005, but a similar dispute then emerged in relation to the French company Compagnie. In light of such attempts to 'appropriate' Rooibos, various efforts have been undertaken to apply GI status to Rooibos and hence to give control over the name to actors in the place where it is grown, South Africa, but more specifically the Northern Cape region's fynbos biome. This is, however, no simple matter. Protecting the name Rooibos and associating it with fair trade status has raised the market value of the crop, but 98% of the crop comes from large farms (1500–2000 hectares) and these are predominantly owned by white farmers. Predominantly non-white small-scale farmers find it harder to meet the new regulations for organic and fair trade status. Almost all processing is undertaken by a small number of dominant processing companies (the largest one taking 70% of all crops), and again these big players receive almost all the overseas earnings (Coombe et al. 2014b). Movements to institute land reform and to help small farmers and cooperatives receive a greater share of the GIs value added require a challenge to the image of the region as a harmonious and organic community, even as the 'social imaginary' of the GI promotes this idyllic misconception. The attempt to deploy global IPRs to promote local prod-ucts and production overwhelmingly advantages those local players already keyed into global economic, legal and linguistic networks – and these tend to be white farmers and factory owners.

A final twist in the tail of the Rooibos GI lies in the impact of climate change on the fynbos biome itself. Rising temperatures, drought and a subsequent decline in pollinating insects in the fynbos mean the place where Rooibos grows is migrating south. Coombe et al. (2014b) suggest this means the Rooibos GI needs to be geographically flexible. GIs are designed to remove geographical dislocation, but global climate change is moving the very ground out from under the feet of those fighting to fix it.

This question of shifting place is not unique to Rooibos and takes us into the realm of traditional and indigenous knowledge within a global network world (discussed in Chapter 4). GI protection from displacing a product that itself migrated to the place now claiming it is problematic. Current placement is very often the result of prior displacement, not resistance to displacement. Some things can be said to be 'indigenous' (at least relative to the span of human agriculture), but even when this claim is not disputed, problems of place can still arise.

If GIs tend to be controlled by powerful actors within their designated places, and if the success of GIs depends on the ability of such actors to use wider networks of business and communication to control product and place, it will be very hard indeed for already displaced and marginalized people to successfully use GIs to overcome their marginality. On its own, protecting place within the space of flows (Castells 2000a, 2000b) of global network capitalism may simply enable local elites to better integrate with global forces. As Coombe et al. (2014a) and Darch (2014a) point out, it is only through wider networks of empowerment and movements towards equity that GIs can serve to improve rather than simply reproduce local inequalities in new globalizing conditions.

DESIGN OBJECTS

'Designer labels' and 'designer goods' typically refer to trademarks that are names. That named person has rarely designed these objects. Most haute couture brand names are the names of founders, not the actual designers working for these 'houses' today. Most such houses are owned by TNCs retaining the original names for recognition and status. As such, 'designer' brands are most often protected under trademark, not under any specific IP protection afforded for 'design' as such.

Design law is ambiguous, siting somewhere between copyright and patent or, increasingly, not siting anywhere at all. Protection of industrial designs (objects of mass production) has been set apart from 'artistic' works as well as from inventions in some jurisdictions (e.g. UK/US and Germany) because of (a) concerns that protecting mass-produced industrial objects with utilitarian functions would be unduly restrictive of industrial competition and development; (b) the belief that mass-produced functional objects are composed out of necessity rather than substantial creative/inventive steps; and (c) the making of such objects is mechanical rather than manual craft work.

While the Berne Convention extends rights over 'applied arts', it also gives states power to determine how far copyright should be extended over functional objects. The same ambivalence can be found in the Paris Convention covering industrial property (Suthersanen 2014). As Adrian Johns (2009) details, debates in the 19th century over IPRs split industrialists on the question of what was in their own best interests. Free access to innovations was attractive – enabling free use of new ideas, yet protection was also attractive if you could secure for yourself more than others could prohibit you from accessing by the same rules.

The case of industrial design law (and whether or not industrial designs should be afforded normal copyright/patent protection) illustrates Bruno Latour's (2005, 7) contention that social structures (and interests) do not simply shape laws and technical assemblages. Rather, in uncertain anticipation of what might come to pass, various actors align and oppose one another.

In time certain alliances may consolidate around particular outcomes. Competing actors may come together around a specific legal or technical configuration which itself then binds their interests together. It may come to appear that these common interests preceded and 'caused' the legal/technical outcome. The opposite may be just as much the case.

Suthersanen documents that in the UK industrial objects are deemed less original than pure creative art works. Protection extends for only 25 years (at best), rather than life plus 70 years as it does on copyrighted works. In Germany, the concept of 'Spielraum' (room to play) was used to suggest that functional objects – having fewer 'degrees of freedom' in the relationship between functional necessity and creative originality – should not be given equal protection as pure creative works receive. However, Suthersanen notes French law has tended to apply a non-discriminatory approach between pure and applied arts. Different jurisdictions have made different decisions regarding the balance between rewarding innovation and limiting monopolies over functional objects, creating different affordances as much as reflecting different sets of prior interests. UK/US laws have allowed those countries to become centres for 'reproduction' furniture (making copies of famous designer items afforded no protection), while France's greater protection of designs may have enabled as much as simply reflected existing strengths in this area.

Nonetheless, pressures towards harmonization exist, even as laws remain contradictory. The Court of Justice of the European Union (CJEU) determined in 2011 that the 2001 Community Design Regulation (CDR) was retroactive in offering protection to designs created before the regulation's agreement. The 2011 judgement was in relation to copies made of the 1962 Italian design classic Arco Lamp and determined that not only should industrial designs be accorded equal status with fine art works but that such equality should be retrospective – and so apply to works designed as far back as the 1962 Arco design. The CDR's 2001 suspension of the distinction between industrial and craft production and between utility and aesthetic purpose, in line with prior French law, incorporated industrial design within copyright law, but individual states continued to exercise discretion in applying it.

The Court of Justice decision in 2011 rejected the view that the CDR's 2001 rules were merely optional. The UK prime minister's wife's choice to buy (legally under UK law) a reproduction Arco Lamp to decorate number 10 Downing Street in the same year as the CJEU decision to prohibit such reproduction Arco lamps (Morris 2011) indicates continued divergence. While Germany has revised its law and has come into line with France and the CDR, the UK continues to stand out.

Suthersanen (2014, 550–551) also uses the 2011 case of *Lucasfilm Ltd v. Ainsworth* to highlight the distinctions between copyrightable art and uncopyrightable design. In this case, Lucasfilm claimed copyright over the storm trooper helmet designs used in the *Star Wars* franchise. Andrew Ainsworth, the 'original maker' of the helmets for Lucasfilm, also claimed ownership. A US court found in favour of Lucasfilm, on the premise that the helmets were made as works for hire and hence copyrightable by Ainsworth's employer – Lucasfilm. The UK courts found the helmets to be functional, not works of art, and thus not protected by copyright. While unable to prevent injury in a space laser battle (and so not functional at that level) the helmets were seen as props and thus 'useful'. As a result, neither party were awarded copyright, but rather a design protection of 15 years was established. Ainsworth could thus sell 'original maker' helmets, made from the original cast, but replicas produced by others could also be legally available. Given the helmets had first been made in 1976 (Bowcott 2011), the 15-year design protection had already elapsed by 2011 when the legal dispute emerged.

In 2011, the UK continued to uphold the distinction between art and function, copyright and design. As Suthersanen concludes (2014, 555), while the US and UK continue to allow a free-market in 'unauthorized reproductions' (though US courts are more favourable to US applicants), Germany and Italy have 'harmonized' with France in equalizing industrial designs with copyrightable creations. The US and UK attend more to promoting and extending copyright and patent. Continental Europe has pressed harder towards extending protections for designs and GIs in line with levels of protection given for copyright and patent. Global negotiations – even when dominated by elites – cannot be assumed to be foregone conclusions. Latour is right, that we should interrogate how networks form precisely because they could have been (and can become) otherwise. Noting the tensions and contradictions among those who would harmonize and extend IPRs is important as it highlights their fragile contingency, despite their seeming omnipotence in today's global network capitalism.

CONCLUSIONS

Within global network capitalism, trademarks are used to bind corporate ownership and control over globally outsourced production and stand in contrast to GIs, which are used to bind production to particular locations ('insourcing' if you will). However, both function to control the supply of 'authentic' goods and hence to enable higher (monopoly) prices. Trademarks and GIs 'mark' origin, by either company or geography, but their 'social imaginaries' say nothing (necessarily) about the actual conditions of production or the quality of the product.

Such 'social imaginaries' may in fact contribute to misrepresentation. Global networks of moral regulation (brand citizenship) seek to use global networks of legal (IP) regulation as conduits to raise labour, environmental and quality standards and to link consumers to producers more directly. Such campaigns seek to expose what global network capitalist outsourcing and brand management may obscure. Global networks of moral deregulation (pirate/counterfeit capitalism) seek to use global networks of supply, outsourced production and distribution to profit from reduced prices. Counterfeit consumer culture embraces reduced costs as 'democratic' participation (an inverted form of 'brand citizenship'), against regulations that exclude the poorer consumer.

The tension within global network capitalism is then one between deregulated markets and the regulation of property rights. Transnational firms have pressed for deregulation (and hence free-markets) in labour and production while at the same time pressing for regulation (in the form of monopoly controls) over trademarks (as they have for copyright and patent). GIs (as shown above) have been taken up by continental European elites against what is perceived to be excessive deregulation of markets led by US/UK free-marketeers. GIs have also been used elsewhere to similar ends. Ironically, the drive towards global 'harmonization' of IP regimes (such as over trademark) sees global firms, often themselves at the forefront of promoting deregulation in labour and production, demanding regulation against pirates and counterfeiters whose 'free' marketeering is said to be too 'free' in bypassing the (IP) rights of dominant actors.

As the case of design law indicated, tensions remain among elites in different countries as to how to balance interests in free competition and those in protecting property rights in practical knowledge. While attempts to extend regulation over 'their' (property) rights, while campaigning to deregulate the (labour) rights of others, might be seen as straightforwardly self-interested hypocrisy, disputes between elites within and between states over competing interpretations and expectations regarding the benefits and dangers of protectionism and competition show that self-interest is never as straightforward a thing to calculate and hence act upon.

6

CONCLUSIONS AND PARADOXES

As was noted in Chapter 1 of this book, IP arose with the development of early capitalism. Today's global network capitalism, to the extent that it can, constructs and defends global IP, just as earlier forms of capitalism reconfigured and defended the idea of physical 'property' at first the national and then at the international level. Earlier formations of capitalism had to first alienate 'property' from prior configurations of access, obligation and control over land, craft and exchange and then defend such property rights against contrary rights claims being made by subordinate classes. Central to earlier defences of property were economic claims that asserted private property's confluence of efficiency and incentive, combined with legal philosophies that asserted private property's combination of incentive with 'natural' justice and, of course, physical force. As this book has shown, the fabrication of claims firstly for IP and more recently for the global extension of IP follows similar lines, and these claims are just as self-serving and inconsistent as their predecessors.

Global IP expansion acts to maintain today's global network society as global network capitalism. As this book has argued, such a global configuration of IPRs is not a natural or necessary outcome. The WTO, TRIPS and WIPO, while primarily focused on the task of protecting IP at the same time as undoing other forms of regulation, have encountered challenges from an array of actors internal to their structures (in particular developing states) who resist this agenda. As such, alternative treaty mechanisms have been set in play to bypass such resistance and attempt to further expand IPR protection globally. Some have stalled, like the ACTA, and others have come forward to take their place, most recently the TPP and the TTIP. The regulatory mechanisms set in place to manage global network capitalism have not proved a one-way street in rolling out ownership in the world of ideas.

Beyond the regulatory agencies and treaty negotiations themselves, global network society has not simply given in to attempts to extend IP. Here a particularly acute paradox can be observed. On the one hand, to the extent that physical labour and production are devalued while immaterial capital is protected via copyright, patents, trademarks, etc., the value of informational commodities can be maintained and ever greater profit can be drawn from information-rich goods. Costs fall and markets expand. The physical carrier of such IP-rich content (a CD, DVD, branded t-shirt or pill) becomes increasingly cheap to mass-produce by means of automation and/or outsourcing. As long as IP holders can regulate and exert control over the informational content, this content can command a relatively high price, even as the production costs (and prices) fall away. Technological automation/outsourcing can even make the customer/end-user do the labour by 'making' the copy themselves, even while paying the IP owner for access to content.

On the other hand, unlike purchasing a car, which cannot be easily copied, when selling or outsourcing content, even if what is being 'sold' is access to the content, the buyer still 'acquires' a copy. As a copy of the IP-protected immaterial content is in fact a copy of the IP itself, the buyer is acquiring not just a product but the means of further production as well. It is one thing to pass ever tighter laws asserting that the global network capitalist enterprise retains ownership over the content it 'sells' to customers. It is quite another to say that those laws overcome the fundamental fact that whereas in the past a company making shoes would sell shoes and keep the capital necessary for making more shoes, now IPR holding enterprises sell copies of content that are themselves sufficient or very nearly sufficient for making further copies. However, the law is imposed to ensure that no further copies are made by the consumer or shared without authorization. In a purified version of global network capitalism, all sharing would be eliminated and all copies purchased individually from the IP owner. Thankfully, the global network society is very far from such an uninhibited property-based regime. Global network society is far more than just global network capitalism.

Given the ease with which products whose value rests in IP and its legal protections can be copied and reproduced, and the fact that from a single purchased product comes the possibility of further production, such products are by definition insecure. While such insecurity plays out very differently in relation to copyright goods and to patent/trademarked goods, at least in terms of how such IP 'leaks' out, in all cases the extension of IPRs via global networks is never as secure as the law asserts and IP defenders would wish. For example, while agribusiness companies build 'terminator genes' into seeds to limit seed fertility, such behaviour has been heavily resisted by farmers throughout the world. Parallel attempts to build encryption into digital content have failed outright. Finally, it is precisely the simplicity of global trademark identifiers that, while making them recognizable in the first place, also makes them utterly impossible to prevent from being easily copied.

As we move into an uncertain future, it is always worth considering how current disputes and possibilities concerning the ownership of ideas might unfold. There are numerous problems, tensions and paradoxes within today's global IP regime. These existing pressures, along with future, as-yet-unknown technical affordances and social processes, may lead to radical changes. The final sections of this conclusion reflect upon the consequent fragility of IP and ownership in the world of ideas.

EXTENSION AND/OR FRAGMENTATION?

As has been documented throughout this book, expansion has been central to IP's history. Such expansion can be seen across three dimensions – those of time, space and depth. Expansion, in principle, could refer to extension of coverage in terms of the duration of the protection afforded, the geographical reach such protection covers, and/or in terms of the depth of what is deemed protected (both in the kinds of things that could be covered and how far one thing has to resemble another to be deemed an infringement of it).

Across these three dimensions of potential extension, change has occurred over time. This change is neither linear nor identical in relation to different types of IP. Copyright, patent, trademarks and GIs have all evolved differently in their specifics, even as protection of IP in general has followed a logic of expansion. In essence, the rise of global network capitalism in the last three decades has been premised upon and has then driven forward an expansion of IP coverage, even as expansion has been neither uniform nor entirely without resistance and reversal.

Copyright has witnessed perhaps the most radical expansion across all three dimensions, with duration of protection extensions, to between 50 and 70 years beyond the death of the 'author', being written into law by all signatories to the WTO's TRIPS agreement. TRIPS has now been signed by almost all states recognized by the UN. At the same time, what is deemed covered (in terms of depth of coverage) has also expanded with 'look and feel' now being sufficient to generate copyright protection. Where once a film based on a book was not seen to infringe that book, today that film would be considered a 'derivative work' even if the visual and audible expression is clearly different from a written text.

Regarding patent, extension in time has been more limited, with little movement in the last three decades in the actual duration of protection afforded to patent holders. However, 'evergreening' allows minor alterations to enable 'new' patent applications to effectively extend old ones. The scope of geographical protection has changed, however, with TRIPS members now required to defend the patent claims of foreign IP holders. Depth of coverage has also expanded radically with legal decisions that allow patent claims over naturally occurring organisms and processes if they can be synthesized/abstracted from nature.

Regarding trademarks and GIs, time was never limited as long as holders renewed their claims, and this has not changed. Again, as with copyright and patent, what has most radically altered is the jurisdictional expansion of trademark enforcement. Trademark owners are no longer limited to their national jurisdictions, but can press claims globally. In addition, and similarly again to copyright and patent, there has been a radical rise in the depth of coverage – most notably in relation to GIs which have proliferated in recent years and have now been secured on a far wider array of place-specific products.

Across the three fields of IP discussed above, it is clear that geographical reach and depth of coverage have formally expanded in each case, even while time extension has only really been significant in relation to copyright. However, this 'formal' extension must be set against an array of limits and resistances. As noted in Chapter 1, global network capitalism is riven with contradictions. Globalization extends markets but also extends the flow of valuable ideas beyond the full control of legal owners. This is only further exacerbated by network technologies. Capitalism itself is conflicted between a desire to defend the monopoly control of property and the desire to promote free- and open-market competition. Unlawfully, free 'pirate' capitalism, as discussed in Chapter 5, is the most extreme manifestation of free-market competition breaching monopoly prohibitions and undermining established monopoly players.

Global networks create a dialectic between their capitalist and social affordances. On the one hand, global network capitalism extends IPRs globally because without such legal protection products where the content is easily copyable are globally vulnerable. Informational goods contain within themselves the possibility of their own reproduction because the copy of the product is the capital itself. As such, every recipient of such a product, whether that be the end-user or an outsourced manufacturer, acquires enough 'capital' to go into direct competition with the 'lawful' supplier by simply reproducing copies. Such copies may be 'pirate' copies for sale or free copies to share. From the point of view of the IP owner, how unauthorized copies are distributed is not the primary concern. That any unauthorized copying undermines their economic control over content distribution is what is at stake.

The extension of IPRs globally and increasing regulation right down to the level of every individual customer across the world might seem like a manifestation of a new and powerful 'world order' (a global big brother watching everyone), yet the reverse is equally true. Such a totalizing regime of regulation – targeting everyone everywhere – also reflects the fact that global network capitalism is now threatened by everyone everywhere. In the past, copying and illegal reproductions were only a threat posed by the relatively small number of alternative manufacturers who had the same ability to make and distribute products as rights holders did. Today, global networks level the playing field and it is this increased vulnerability, not simply unchecked power, that compels the kinds of global regulation that has been rolled out. Yet, such roll-out has neither stopped mass infringement of copyright-protected works by sharers, nor prevented trademark-protected products from being produced and sold by commercial counterfeiters using the very same factories that IP holders use in globally outsourcing production, nor ended government-licenced patent-infringing generic drugs manufacture in the global south.

There is a yawning gap between the de jure extension of law in principle and the ability to enforce law (de facto) in real life. This is most manifest in relation to copyright, which is itself the form of IP most radically extended in recent years. Similarly, a gap has emerged within the very multilateral (global) organizations created to regulate IP enforcement. In incorporating almost all nations within their frameworks, WTO, TRIPS and WIPO have swallowed up the whole world, yes, but they have not yet digested it. These forums have seen resistance and alternatives proposed by many member countries from within the global south. Recent developments in South America, South Africa and South Asia – where, for example, governments are pressing ahead with the production of generic drugs to deal with domestic and international health emergencies – show that while the world is integrated through global political and economic regimes, it is far from pacified or homogeneous. The very structure of international organizations along the democratic lines of one country one vote means that internally all today's multilateral IP forums remain fragmented, and IP hotly debated.

While bilateral agreements are being developed to contain the rebellions that have arisen within the multilateral fora originally designed to regulate the globe in the interests of IP holders, an even more significant challenge is emerging across global networks – the rise of the 3D printer revolution. As noted above, the most extreme extension of IP has come in relation to copyright, in part because this domain has been most radically challenged by infringement since digital technologies make it possible for every networked citizen on the planet to copy the IP of rights holders. Within the fields of patent and trademark IP infringement still requires a manufacturing base. However, it is the case that global network capitalism, by outsourcing most of its physical production of IP-rich goods to the global south, has made counterfeit manufacturing far easier and more widespread because both pirated goods and 'official' goods are now produced in the same places, but follow different distribution chains. Nonetheless, the 3D printer revolution offers the very immanent prospect of abolishing that distinction. In the very near future, every citizen will be able to copy IP-rich physical goods (handbags, medicines and gadgets) as easily as they can now copy songs, films and computer games.

GLOBAL IPR'S – INCENTIVE OR INHIBITOR TO INNOVATION?

A second question that remains relevant today is the extent to which global IPRs incentivize or inhibit innovation. The point of IPRs is to limit the supply of the protected item such that the rights holder can command a price higher than if there was an open market in the item's supply. IP is designed to inflate prices above market rates. Such monopoly rent is a burden upon consumers, but is said to be a price worth paying if the inflated price provides the incentive for the product so priced to have been made available in the first place. A high price for something is always better than nothing, as some will afford it while those unable to afford that price would not have had access to the product anyway if it did not exist. If a lower price would mean the innovation was never developed and made available in the first place, then extending a monopoly is justified.

As was noted in Chapter 3, economists point out that even if IP did not incentivize production of novel works in the first place, they may well provide the incentive for commercial actors to distribute them (Phythian-Adams 2014). If this were ever true, it would be very unlikely to hold much sway today when global networks afford far more efficient distribution of information-rich content than can be offered by commercial actors – actors who defend IP precisely because they cannot compete with such ('free-riding'/'free-market') alternatives. As such, IP's defence cannot be on grounds of being necessary to encourage distribution in an age of near-frictionless global networks. IP's defence therefore must rely on a demonstration that they do indeed incentivize rather than inhibit innovation.

As also discussed in Chapter 3, the argument for IP-promoting innovation is questionable at best. In the case of music, the standard IP/royalties model proved (and continues to prove) a highly ineffective means of rewarding artists – with most ending up owing their record companies money because their contracts are so exploitative. Those artists who make money from music do so mainly from live performance, not from recording, and those who do make money from recording very, very rarely make more from recording than they do from live performance. The collapse in the sale of recorded music with the rise of file-sharing saw a sharp increase in money spent on live performance. As such, the bypassing of copyright protection by fans simply file-sharing or streaming music for free has been good news for artists.

For movies, a similar argument can be made. Downloading has not reduced cinema attendance and in ways encouraged it, even if file-sharing challenges the traditional distribution model where content moved in a controlled fashion from the theatre to home rental and finally on to television. Still, the bypassing of copyright in this creative sector has not spelt the end of creativity or productivity in film. Computer games makers thrive by being one step ahead of those who would pirate their products, not by enforcing IP on dated products that have outlived their shelf life. Being purely digital makes games totally open to infringement, and it is the lack of effective security that makes the sector so very much more dynamic than older media industries (like music and film).

That all digital rights management software created by corporate programmers has been broken by open source hackers also suggests that innovation is better achieved through sharing than by proprietary control. Just as musicians have found better ways of getting paid by connecting with their audiences rather than trying to force them into paying for content, so it is that writers are better off connecting with and encouraging fan appropriations of their work rather than trying to use copyright to pacify their readers.

Trademarks and GIs make no claim to be seeking to incentivize innovation. They are designed primarily to reward prior work. As was noted in Chapter 5, it is a misconception to believe that trademarks actually guarantee the quality of a product. They only ensure the identity of the formal owner of the mark; they do not say anything meaningful about the actual physical producer of the product under trademark, let alone the composition of the product itself. GIs are said to reward some prior (often presented as primordial) invention, but this is, like trademark, to reward preservation not innovation. As such, while the case for copyright-promoting innovation is problematic, there simply is no case made when it comes to trademarks and GIs.

What then of patents? A starving artist may create for the love of their art and then make a living busking for donations (the very metaphor used by successful artists such as Courtney Love and Radiohead when arguing they are better paid via voluntary tips for downloads and the choice of buying a concert ticket than from the – often non-existent – royalties offered in exchange for signing over copyright to a record company). The image of modern pharmaceuticals and the agribusiness stands in stark contrast to this. Big science needs big – upfront – investment in high-risk research that may never lead to a useful product. Surely a sufficient incentive needs to be created – in terms of lucrative monopoly control over what does work – to enable innovation to take place. Is that right?

In reality, the situation is rather more murky and complex. As was seen in the case of AZT, this HIV-inhibiting drug was developed by a combination of charitable funding, university research, government-funded laboratories and a private sector company that got involved with trialling the drug only once it reached a stage where it looked like it might become a promising (i.e. profitable) medication. Once developed, AZT has been patented and sold as though it were the result solely of private rights holder's investment. This is a gross simplification and a deeply problematic one. Since the development of AZT, research into more effective medications that can deal with AIDS rather than HIV have followed a similar narrative of collaboration among state, university, charity and commercial actors, with the latter always keen to capitalize on the outcomes, but very reluctant to share what they themselves find for fear that such information might benefit their competitors when it comes to patenting and selling the end results. Patent thickets, secrecy and non-collaboration, not bold upfront investment, characterize the involvement of private companies in innovation. The 2014–2015 outbreak of Ebola in West Africa is also illustrative. Research into this virus languished for years as its victims were largely poor and unable to pay for treatment. Only when it looked like Ebola was spreading beyond West Africa did western governments step up the pace of research. Once the virus became a priority for western states, these states' disease control agencies fast-tracked and funded rapid trials, while non-commercial agencies intervened to ensure supplies could be distributed. Private companies are in fact deeply risk-averse and look to non-commercial actors to underwrite their investments even when, after the fact, they will seek to claim ownership over what can generate a profit for them.

While the most speculative 'blue-sky' research is funded upstream by non-commercial actors, commercial actors like to claim they are the ones taking all the risks, which is a serious misrepresentation of how research is accomplished. This 'risk' taking claim is used to justify existing patent protection and, when no new drug arrives to replace the one currently on the market, for further extensions of the existing patent (an agenda item in current TTIP and TPP negotiations). In reality such further extensions of protection would increase disincentives to innovate and reward preservation/rent-seeking; it would exacerbate the patent thickets that block further innovation and would work to continue freezing out alternative suppliers (such as the burgeoning generics industry in the global south).

Will a thriving generics market kill off innovation in the pharmaceutical sector? Or rather, would reducing the scope for monopoly rent promote innovation, as Big Pharma in developed states is no longer able to sit on long-term global monopolies covering past breakthroughs? Will increased competition lead pharmaceutical companies to innovate faster and better? No doubt this would require working in new ways, greater collaboration (beyond patent thickets and secrecy) and will require more equity in dealings between commercial actors and the state agencies, charities and university research laboratories that already made great contributions to innovation, but whose work is currently bought up and hived off into private hands. Perhaps more competition between commercial actors and more equitable cooperation with non-commercial ones would be no bad thing and so should be welcomed. As such, the case for patents is no more robust than that for copyright as a mechanism for incentivizing innovation, and that is not very robust at all.

The link between innovation and IP is an area of research of great interest to numerous scholars and a growing field of inquiry. Jessica Silbey has been interviewing cultural, technical and scientific innovators across all fields of IP for many years. Her findings suggest a very large gap between the creative incentives that actually motivate innovation and the justifications for and incentives created by IP law (Silbey 2014). Silbey's work supports the view that creators value their moral rights to be known for their contribution, but the suggestion that they are motivated by exclusive monopoly control on what they themselves create is rarely true. That scientists who work for corporations, or musicians signed to record labels, do not end up really owning their creations anyway reinforces this view – that creators are not motivated by ownership – precisely because they do not own outcomes in any substantive sense. That the corporations which do end up owning rights to reproduce the work of scientists, musicians and writers claim their employees/artists are so motivated is therefore doubly misleading.

While the possibility of profit from exclusive use can motivate some, it is not an all-encompassing rational, nor even the primary rational for innovation. Rather, it is often an afterthought. Academics gain from acknowledgement and citation and so largely write for nothing and promote free distribution of their work whenever possible. Payment is truly an afterthought. If you do not believe us – read the contract with our publishers! Artists produce true art for themselves and other artists. Only later do they worry about making a living, which usually involves diluting their original innovations in order to satisfy a paying (i.e. 'philistine') audience. When an artist becomes 'commercial' this is usually understood to mean when they cease to be genuinely original. Inventors are often caught up in the excitement of new ideas, not how to make money from them. Whether they work for states, charities, universities or private firms, the IP implications of their work are not central to their creativity. Of the above examples, only commercial artists may be specifically motivated by IP monopoly rent-seeking. Claims that IP produces the highest levels of innovation is exaggerated at best and is, at worse, simply false. As Timothy Wu's (2011) excellent analysis of the history of innovation in the field of communication technology indicates, innovation occurs beyond IP and then IP is used as a blunt instrument to control access to ideas.

GLOBAL IPR'S – FOR OR AGAINST JUSTICE, SUSTAINABILITY AND DEVELOPMENT?

Given the global attention now paid to all forms of IPRs, rights holders and supportive governments are increasingly under scrutiny by those critical of how IP has been conceptualized and enforced. Such scrutiny and often outright protest means that IP owners have sought to frame ownership in terms of enhancing human welfare and development. WIPO, for example, as a special agency of the UN, must align its mission with that of development, which led many countries and non-governmental actors to call for a 'development agenda' within WIPO to better assess how expansive IP laws impact development. Now that the development agenda has been set in place, it remains to be seen if these new assessment measures will have any meaningful impact on development throughout the global south.

Outside WIPO, new bilateral and multilateral treaties have also sparked protest as have IP expansionists' claims that such protections are necessary for improving human well-being. We must, expansionists argue, have better protection against counterfeiting because illegally produced drugs and autoparts can kill. Thus, IP owners attempt to frame even more restrictive IP laws as necessary to preserve human health, enhance development and spark the necessary innovation to save the environment. Critics point out that it is IP monopoly prices that drive the market for counterfeits in the first place, limit technology transfer and encourage ongoing dependence on outdated eco-unfriendly technologies in countries that are priced out of adopting cleaner alternatives, and that it is the IP protectionist lobby itself that seeks to confuse the important distinction between 'real' generic drugs and substantively 'fake' counterfeit ones as this suits their interests even as it harms those of consumers.

As discussed in Chapter 4, while patents certainly figure in the control of technologies that will have an impact on human health and welfare, and on technologies that might contribute to the fight against global warming, it is in no way clear that patent protection caused such technologies to exist. Additionally, sharing knowledge under patent protection remains problematic, and despite claims that IP will promote technology transfer, there remains little evidence of such practices. Rather, controlling access to life-saving medicine and technologies and making such things available only to those who can afford to pay their monopoly prices, all the while fighting against possible safe and afford-able generic versions, suggests an approach that places profit well above solving human suffering or environmental problems. Patents, in other words, put profits first, and only if the fee demanded has been paid is it possible to think about the benefit to humanity. If these fees are not paid, resultant suffering and loss are not accepted to be the patent holders' problem or responsibility. As such IP protectionists 'externalize' moral responsibility while internalizing benefits, just as they seek to externalize costs (when taking advantage of TK and the work of charities, universities and state-funded research agencies) even while then seeking to take credit for (internalizing) any resulting innovation.

SUMMARY

The future has yet to be written. As such, it is important to explore possible alternatives, including, but not limited to, the perpetual ratcheting up of IP protection. Certainly, if one were to speculate about the future of IP based upon its current statuary trajectory, given that IP now spans the entire globe, it seems likely that formal expansion will continue in terms of length of protec-tion, geographical reach and/or depth of protection. However, because there remain countries, activists, scholars, file-sharers and citizens around the world who envision and perform in their everyday practices alternatives to perpetual extension, the dominant narrative remains deeply insecure, and it is worthwhile to sketch the possible alternative futures that could prevail.

One possible future follows upon the demands of the global south and anti-IP activists to forestall ongoing attempts to further extend IP, while a second is even to significantly roll back past extensions. In the case of the former, the failure of ACTA stands out as a significant victory in blocking off further exten-sion, while the development agenda within the WTO and WIPO is another. Protest against TTIP and TPP is yet further evidence of the non-inevitability of ever deeper, longer and wider ownership over the world of ideas.

Beyond the prevention of further roll-out is actual roll-back, as has been seen in the recalibration debates within WIPO/TRIPS and in the legalization of a swathe of generic drugs across the global south. A further step in this roll-back agenda would be to reset copyright protection at a much more limited term. Rather than protecting copyright for the life of the author plus 50 or 70 years, for example, a fixed term of 14 years could be set. Mickey Mouse would be 'freed' and the Disney Corporation might be inspired to think up something new.

A third possible future might be the abolition of IP altogether. IP monopolies are inconsistent with the idea of a free-market economy. If indeed the globe is to embrace free-market ideology, then it ought to abolish monopolies that disrupt the free flow of goods and especially ideas. Such 'free' and 'open' access to western markets and technology remain denied to poorer countries in the global south. Given the vast disparities that continue to exist, and which IP monopolies bolster, not all countries see IP protection as essential to their future economic development, and many see it as antithetical. Given the growing pressure to suspend IP in many sectors, one possible future might be an 'ordo-liberal' (anti-trust) dismantling of 'neo-liberalism's' regulative infrastructure (TRIPS in particular). Such an 'ordered liberalism' (as mentioned in Chapter 1) uses regulation to prevent undue monopoly power, as distinct from 'neo-liberalism's' regulation that offers protectionism for the powerful and only uses market deregulation to discipline the poor.

Furthermore, a fourth scenario presents itself. As file-sharing has illustrated, most people who can access the internet have now become accustomed to on-demand entertainment and access to knowledge at a level never seen before. To these end-users, the legality of the access is not as critical as being able to tap into the global flow of human culture. Thus, within global network society, the flow of products will continue to wash over the regulative mechanisms of the state and global governance structures. If you want to download free TV, order generic drugs online and buy 'knock off' handbags at the local market, there is really nothing to stop you. The 3D printers will move this reality on apace. Such a future would see the state playing the role of enforcer of the unenforceable, engaged in an ever more expensive and futile defence of the indefensible. In this scenario, it is not that IP law is either prevented from expansion, or rolled back, or even abolished, but simply rendered irrelevant.

The future is not what it used to be. Neither is the future cut and dried. What this work has sought to show is that ongoing expansion of ownership in the world of ideas is neither inevitable, nor necessary, nor desirable. The contradictions for IP that exist within the global, digital networks and in the capitalist nature of today's society, combined with the willingness of human actors to contest power and create alternatives, means that the drivers towards ongoing IP extension do not have everything their own way. Nor should they.

REFERENCES

Albini, Steve. 1994. The problem with music. *Maximum Rock and Roll* 133. http://www.mpg.org.uk/knowledge-bank/the-problem-with-music-by-steve-albini Accessed 3 May 2015.

Alexander, Isabella. 2007. Criminalising copyright: a story of publishers, pirates and pieces of eight. *Cambridge Law Journal* 66(3): 625–656.

Álvarez, Lillian. 2014. Author and cultural rights: the Cuban case. In David, Matthew and Debora J. Halbert (eds) *The Sage Handbook of Intellectual Property*. London, UK and Los Angeles, CA: Sage, 279–299.

Antons, Christoph. 2009. *Traditional Knowledge, Traditional Cultural Expressions, and Intellectual Property Law in the Asia-Pacific Region*. Alphen Aan Den Rijn, the Netherlands and Frederick, MD: Kluwer Law International and Aspen Publishers.

Association of Research Libraries. 2014. Copyright timeline: a history of copyright in the United States. http://www.arl.org/focus-areas/copyright-ip/2486-copyright-timeline#.VKcoF4ebFyc Accessed 29 April 2015.

Baddache, Farid. 2008. *Procter & Gamble: Providing Safe Drinking Water to the Poor*. GIM Case Study No. A036. New York, NY: United Nations Development Program. http://growinginclusivemarkets.org/media/cases/Developing%20Countries_P&G_2008.pdf

Baker, Dean. 2014. Election results indicate huge mandate for new trade pacts. *The Huffington Post*, 10 November. http://www.huffingtonpost.com/dean-baker/election-results-indicate_b_6136660.html

Barraclough, Emma. 2013. What myriad means for biotech. *WIPO Magazine*, August. http://www.wipo.int/wipo_magazine/en/2013/04/article_0007.html

Barron, Anne. 2014. Intellectual property and the 'open' (information) society. In David, Matthew and Debora J. Halbert (eds) *The Sage Handbook of Intellectual Property*. London, UK and Los Angeles, CA: Sage, 5–27.

Basheer, Shamnad and Annalisa Primi. 2008. *The WIPO Development Agenda: Factoring in the "Technologically Proficient" Developing Countries*. SSRN Scholarly Paper ID 1289288. Rochester, NY: Social Science Research Network. http://papers.ssrn.com/abstract=1289288

Biagioli, Mario. 2011. Patent specification and political representation. In Biagioli, Mario, Peter Jaszi, and Martha Woodmansee (eds) *Making and Unmaking Intellectual Property: Creative Production in Legal and Cultural Perspective*. Chicago, IL: University of Chicago Press, 25–39.

Biagioli, Mario, Peter Jaszi, and Martha Woodmansee, eds. 2011. *Making and Unmaking Intellectual Property: Creative Production in Legal and Cultural Perspective*. Chicago, IL: University of Chicago Press.

Bird, Robert. 2008. *The Global Challenge of Intellectual Property Rights*. Cheltenham, UK and Northampton, MA: Edward Elgar.

Birmingham, Jack and Matthew David. 2011. Live-streaming: will football fans continue to be more law abiding than music fans? *Sport in Society* 14(1): 69–80.

Boateng, Boatema. 2011. *The Copyright Thing Doesn't Work Here: Adinkra and Kente Cloth and Intellectual Property in Ghana*. Minneapolis, MN: University of Minnesota Press.

Boldrin, Michele and David K. Levine. 2008. *Against Intellectual Monopoly*. Cambridge, UK: Cambridge University Press.

Bowcott, Owen. 2011. Star Wars costume maker strikes back against Lucasfilm movie empire. *Guardian*, 27 July. http://www.theguardian.com/film/2011/jul/27/star-wars-helmet-court-case

British Phonographic Industry (BPI). 2008. *More Than the Music: The UK Recorded Music Business and Our Society*. London, UK: BPI.

Brown, Ian. 2014. Copyright technologies and clashing rights. In David, Matthew and Debora J. Halbert (eds) *The Sage Handbook of Intellectual Property*. London, UK and Los Angeles, CA: Sage, 567–585.

Bruner, Edward. 1994. Abraham Lincoln as authentic reproduction. *American Anthropologist* 92(2): 27–37.

Burger, Warren E. 1980. Diamond v. Chakrabarty – 447 U.S. 303 (1980). *Justia US Supreme Court Center*, 16 June. http://supreme.justia.com/cases/federal/us/447/303/case.html

Carroll, Michael W. 2005. One for all: the problem of uniformity cost in intellectual property law. *American University Law Review* 55: 845.

Castells, Manuel. 2000a. *The Rise of the Network Society*. Oxford, UK: Blackwell.

Castells, Manuel. 2000b. Materials for an exploratory theory of the network society. *British Journal of Sociology* 51(1): 5–24.

Castells, Manuel. 2009. *Communication Power*. Oxford, UK: Oxford University Press.

Castoriadis, Cornelius. 1987. *The Imaginary Institution of Society*. Cambridge, MA: MIT Press.

Castoriadis, Cornelius. 1997. *World in Fragments: Writings on Politics, Society, Psycho-analysis, and the Imagination*. Palo Alto, CA: Stanford University Press.

Chan, Anita. 2014. *The Promiscuity of Networks: Digital Universalism and Local Farmers in the Information-Age*. Cambridge, MA: MIT Press.

Charles, Dan. 2012. Top Five Myths of Genetically Modified Seeds, Busted. *NPR. org*, 18 October. http://www.npr.org/blogs/thesalt/2012/10/18/163034053/top-five-myths-of-genetically-modified-seeds-busted

Children's Safe Drinking Water Impact. 2014. The P&G Children's Safe Drinking Water program. http://www.csdw.org/csdw/childrens-safe-drinking-water-impact.shtml Accessed 26 November 2014.

Chon, Margaret. 2014. Slow logo: brand citizenship in global value networks. In David, Matthew and Debora J. Halbert (eds) *The Sage Handbook of Intellectual Property*. London, UK and Los Angeles, CA: Sage, 171–188.

Cline, Elizabeth. 2012. *Overdressed: The Shockingly High Cost of Cheap Fashion*. New York, NY: Penguin.

Conley, John M. 2009. Gene patents and the products of nature doctrine. *Chicago-Kent Law Review* 84(January): 109–132.

Coombe, Rosemary J., Sarah Ives, and Daniel Huizenga. 2014a. Geographical indications: the promise, perils and politics of protecting place-based product. In David, Matthew and Debora J. Halbert (eds) *The Sage Handbook of Intellectual Property*. London, UK and Los Angeles, CA: Sage, 207–223.

Coombe, Rosemary J., Sarah Ives, and Daniel Huizenga. 2014b. The social imaginary of geographical indicators in contested environments: the politicized heritage and the racialized landscapes of South African Rooibos Tea. In David, Halbert and Debora J. Halbert (eds) *The Sage Handbook of Intellectual Property*. London, UK and Los Angeles, CA: Sage, 224–237.

Crouch, Colin. 2004. *Post-Democracy*. Cambridge, UK: Polity Press.

Crouch, Colin. 2011. *The Strange Non-Death of Neo-Liberalism*. Cambridge, UK: Polity Press.

Darch, Colin. 2014a. The political economy of traditional knowledge, trademarks and copyright in South Africa. In David, Matthew and Debora J. Halbert (eds) *The Sage Handbook of Intellectual Property*. London, UK and Los Angeles, CA: Sage, 263–278.

Darch, Colin. 2014b. Politics, law and discourse: patents and innovation in post-Apartheid South Africa. In David, Matthew and Debora J. Halbert (eds) *The Sage Handbook of Intellectual Property*. London, UK and Los Angeles, CA: Sage, 631–648.

David, Matthew. 2006. Romanticism, creativity and copyright: visions and nightmares. *European Journal of Social Theory* 9(3): 425–433.

David, Matthew. 2010. *Peer to Peer and the Music Industry: The Criminalization of Sharing*. London, UK: Sage.

David, Matthew. 2011. Music lessons: football finance and live streaming. *Journal of Policy Research in Tourism, Leisure and Events* 3(1): 95–98.

David, Matthew. 2013. Cultural, legal, technical and economic perspectives on copyright online: the case of the music industry. In William H. Dutton (ed.) *The Oxford Handbook of Internet Studies*. Oxford, UK: Oxford University Press, 464–485.

David, Matthew, Amanda Rohloff, Julian Petley, and Jason Hughes. 2011. The idea of moral panic – ten dimensions of dispute. *Crime, Media, Culture* 7(3): 215–228.

David, Matthew, Andrew Kirton, and Peter Millward. 2014. Sports television broadcasting and the challenge of live-streaming. In David, Matthew and Debora J. Halbert (eds) *The Sage Handbook of Intellectual Property*. London, UK and Los Angeles, CA: Sage, 435–450.

David, Matthew and Debora J. Halbert, eds. 2014. *The Sage Handbook of Intellectual Property*. London, UK and Los Angeles, CA: Sage.

David, Matthew and Jamieson Kirkhope. 2004. New digital technologies: privacy/property, globalization and law. *Perspectives on Global Development and Technology* 3(4): 437–449.

David, Matthew and Jamieson Kirkhope. 2006. The impossibility of technical security: intellectual property and the paradox of informational capitalism. In Lacy, Mark and Peter Witkin (eds) *Global Politics in Global Politics in an Information Age*. Manchester, UK: Manchester University Press, 88–95.

David, Matthew and Natasha Whiteman. 2014. 'Piracy' or parody: moral panic in an age of new media. In David, Matthew and Debora J. Halbert (eds) *The Sage Handbook of Intellectual Property*. London, UK and Los Angeles, CA: Sage, 451–469.

David, Matthew and Peter Millward. 2012. Footballs coming home? Digital reterritorialization, contradictions in the transnational coverage of sport and the sociology of alternative football broadcasts. *British Journal of Sociology* 63(2): 349–369.

de Beer, Jeremy. 2009. *Implementing the World Intellectual Property Organization's Development Agenda*. Waterloo, Ontario: Wilfrid Laurier University Press.

Dobbin, Liza and Martin Zeilinger. 2014. Treasuring IP: free culture, media piracy and the international pirate party movement. In David, Matthew and Debora J. Halbert (eds) *The Sage Handbook of Intellectual Property*. London, UK and Los Angeles, CA: Sage, 370–386.

Drahos, Peter. 2003. *Information Feudalism: Who Owns the Knowledge Economy?* New York, NY: New Press.

Drahos, Peter and Ruth Mayne. 2002. *Global Intellectual Property Rights: Knowledge, Access and Development*. Houndmills, UK: Palgrave/Oxfam.

Duffy, John F. 2002. Harmony and diversity in global patent law. *Berkeley Technology Law Journal* 17: 685–726.

Dutfield, Graham. 2006. *Protecting Traditional Knowledge: Pathways to the Future*. Geneva, Switzerland: International Centre for Trade and Sustainable Development (ICTSD).

Dutfield, Graham. 2014. Traditional knowledge, intellectual property and pharma-ceutical innovation: what's left to discuss? In David, Matthew and Debora J. Halbert (eds) *The Sage Handbook of Intellectual Property*. London, UK and Los Angeles, CA: Sage, 649–664.

Edwards, Lee, Bethany Klein, David Lee, Giles Moss, and Fiona Philip. 2013. Framing the consumer: copyright regulation and the public. *Convergence: The International Journal of Research into New Media Technologies* 19(1): 9–24.

Edwards, Lee, Bethany Klein, David Lee, Giles Moss, and Fiona Philip. 2014. Communicating copyright: discourse and disagreement in the digital age. In David, Matthew and Debora J. Halbert (eds) *The Sage Handbook of Intellectual Property*. London, UK and Los Angeles, CA: Sage, 300–314.

Falkvinge, Rick. (2012). Rick Falkvinge: I Am a Pirate. http://www.ted.com/talks/rick_falkvinge_i_am_a_pirate.html Accessed 2 April 2014.

Frank, Robert and Philip Cook. 1996. *The Winner Takes All Society: Why the Few Get so Much More Than the Rest of Us*. New York, NY: Penguin.

Friedman, Milton. 2002. *Capitalism and Freedom*. Chicago, IL: University of Chicago Press.

Fuller, Steve and Veronika Lipinska. 2014. *The Proactionary Imperative: A Foundation for Transhumanism*. London, UK: Palgrave.

Gade, Daniel. 2004. Tradition, territory, and terroir in French viniculture: cassis, France, and appellation contrôlée. *Annals of the Association of American Geographers* 94(4): 848–867.

Gervais, Daniel. 2003. *The TRIPS Agreement: Drafting History and Analysis*. 2nd edition. London, UK: Sweet & Maxwell.

Gervais, Daniel. 2007. *Intellectual Property, Trade and Development: Strategies to Optimize Economic Development in a TRIPS-Plus Era*. Oxford, UK: Oxford University Press. http://econpapers.repec.org/bookchap/oxpobooks/9780199216758.htm

Gervais, Daniel. 2014. TRIPS and development. In David, Matthew and Debora J. Halbert (eds) *The Sage Handbook of Intellectual Property*. London, UK and Los Angeles, CA: Sage, 95–112.

Graber, Christoph. 2008. Using human rights to tackle fragmentation in the field of traditional cultural expressions: an institutional approach. In Graber, Christoph and Muri Burri-Nenova (eds) *Intellectual Property and Traditional Cultural Expressions in Digital Environment*. Cheltenham, UK and Northampton, MA: Edward Elgar, 96–120.

Graber, Christoph and Mira Burri-Nenova. 2008. *Intellectual Property and Traditional Cultural Expressions in a Digital Environment*. Cheltenham, UK and Northampton, MA: Edward Elgar.

Halbert, Debora. 1999. *Intellectual Property in the Information Age: The Politics of Expanding Ownership Rights*. New York, NY: Quorum Books.

Halbert, Debora. 2005. *Resisting Intellectual Property Law*. New York, NY: Routledge.

Halbert, Debora. 2007. The world intellectual property organization: past, present and future. *Journal of the Copyright Society of the USA* 54(2): 253–284.

Halbert, Debora. 2014. *The State of Copyright: The Complex Relationships of Cultural Creation in a Globalized World*. Oxford, UK and New York, NY: Routledge.

Halbert, Debora and Christopher May. 2005. AIDS, pharmaceutical patents and the African State: reorienting the global governance of intellectual property. In Amy Patterson (ed.) *The African State and the AIDS Crisis*. Burlington, VT: Ashgate.

Hauck, Darren. 2014. Supreme Court hands Monsanto victory over farmers on GMO seed patents, ability to sue. *RT USA*, 15 January. http://rt.com/usa/monsanto-patents-sue-farmers-547

Hayek, Frederick. 1946. *The Road to Serfdom*. London, UK: Routledge.

Hegel, Georg Wilhelm Fredrich. 1991. *Hegel: Elements of the Philosophy of Right*. Cambridge, UK: Cambridge University Press.

Held, David. 2010. *Cosmopolitanism: Ideals and Realities*. Cambridge, UK: Polity Press.

Helfer, Laurence and Austin Graeme. 2011. *Human Rights and Intellectual Property: Mapping the Global Interface*. Cambridge, UK: Cambridge University Press.

Hobbes, Thomas. 2008. *Leviathan*. Oxford, UK: Oxford World Classics.

Holmes, Brian. 2003. The emperor's sword: art under WIPO. *World-Information.Org*, December. http://world-information.org/wio/readme/992007035/1078488424

Hughes, Justin. 2012. A short history of 'intellectual property' in relation to copyright. *Cardozo Law Review* 33(4): 1293–1340.

Johns, Adrian. 2009. *Piracy: The Intellectual Property Wars From Gutenberg To Gates*. Chicago, IL: University of Chicago Press.

Johnston, Gordon. 1999. What is the history of Samizdat? *Social History* 24(2): 115–133.

Kirkpatrick, Graeme. 2013. *Computer Games and the Social Imaginary*. Cambridge, UK: Polity.

Kirschbaum, Erik and Irina Ivanova. 2012. Protests erupt across Europe against web piracy treaty. *Reuters*, 11 February. http://www.reuters.com/article/2012/02/11/us-europe-protest-acta-idUSTRE81A0I120120211

Kirton, Andrew. 2014. Music, technology and copyright: the makings and shakings of a global industry. In David, Matthew and Debora J. Halbert (eds) *The Sage Handbook of Intellectual Property*. London, UK and Los Angeles, CA: Sage, 586–606.

Kirton, Andrew and Matthew David. 2013. The challenge of unauthorized online streaming to the English premier league and television broadcasters. In Hutchins, Brett and David Rowe (eds) *Digital Media Sport: Technology, Power and Identity in the Network Society.* Abingdon, UK: Routledge, 81–96.

Klein, Naomi. 2009. *No Logo: Taking Aim at the Brand Bullies.* New York, NY: Macmillan.

Krueger, Alan B. 2004. The economics of real superstars: the market for rock concerts in the material world. *Journal of Labor Economics* 23(1): 1–30. http://dataspace.princeton.edu/jspui/bitstream/88435/dsp016108vb25k/1/484.pdf

Krueger, Alan B. and Marie Connolly. 2006. Rockonomics: the economics of popular music. In Ginsberg, Victor A. and David Throsby (eds) *Handbook of the Economics of Art and Culture.* Amsterdam, the Netherlands: North-Holland, 667–720.

Langshaw, Mark. 2011. Software piracy: the greatest threat to the gaming industry? *Digital Spy.* http://www.digitalspy.co.uk/gaming/news/a352906/software-piracy-the-greatest-threat-to-the-gaming-industry.html#~oTUG5JRRUaQwGb Accessed 27 October 2014.

Larsson, Stefan. 2013. Copy me happy: the metaphoric expansion of copyright in a digital society. *International Journal for the Semiotics of Law* 26: 615–634.

Lastowka, Greg. 2014. Copyright law and video games: a brief history of an interactive medium. In David, Matthew and Debora J. Halbert (eds) *The Sage Handbook of Intellectual Property.* London, UK and Los Angeles, CA: Sage, 495–514.

Latour, Bruno. 2005. *Reassembling the Social.* Oxford, UK: Oxford University Press.

Lee, David. 2012. Europe takes to streets over acta. *BBC News,* 11 February. http://www.bbc.co.uk/news/technology-16999497

Lee, Jyn-An. 2014. Non-profits in the commons economy. In David, Matthew and Debora J. Halbert (eds) *The Sage Handbook of Intellectual Property.* London, UK and Los Angeles, CA: Sage, 335–354.

Leong, Susanna H.S. 2014. Patentable subject matter: a comparative jurisdictional analysis of the discovery/invention dichotomy. In David, Matthew and Debora J. Halbert (eds) *The Sage Handbook of Intellectual Property.* London, UK and Los Angeles, CA: Sage, 665–684.

Lessig, Lawrence. 2004. *Free Culture: How Big Media Uses Technology and the Law to Lock Down and Control Creativity.* New York, NY: Penguin.

Lessig, Lawrence. 2005. *Free Culture: The Nature and Future of Creativity.* New York, NY: Penguin.

Levin, Martin B. 1983. Soviet international copyright: dream or nightmare. *Journal of the Copyright Society of the USA* 31: 127–162.

Liebler, Raizel. 2014. Copyright and ownership of fan created works: fanfiction and beyond. In David, Matthew and Debora J. Halbert (eds) *The Sage Handbook of Intellectual Property.* London, UK and Los Angeles, CA: Sage, 391–403.

Litman, Jessica. 1991. Copyright as Myth. *Pittsburgh Law Review* 53: 235–249.

Locke, John. 1988. *Two Treaties of Government.* Cambridge, UK: Cambridge University Press.

Löhr, Isabella. 2011. Intellectual property rights between nationalization and globalization. Introduction. In Löhr, Isabella and Hannes Siegrist (eds) *Intellectual Property Rights and Globalization.* Leipzig, Germany: Leipziger Universitätsverlag, 27–45.

Phythian-Adams, Sarah Louisa. 2014. The economic foundations of intellectual property: an arts and cultural economist's perspective. In David, Matthew and Debora J. Halbert (eds) *The Sage Handbook of Intellectual Property*. London, UK and Los Angeles, CA: Sage, 28–51.

Love, Courtney. 2000. The Love Manifesto. http://www.indie-music.com/modules. php?name=News&file=article&sid=820 Accessed 3 May 2015.

Lury, Celia. 2004. *Brands: The Logos of the Global Economy*. Abingdon, UK and New York, NY: Routledge.

Marshall, Lee. 2005. *Bootlegging*. London, UK: Sage.

May, Christopher. 2000. *A Global Political Economy of Intellectual Property Rights: The New Enclosures?* London, UK: Routledge.

May, Christopher. 2006. Escaping the trips trap: the political economy of free and open source software in Africa. *Political Studies* 54(1): 123–146.

May, Christopher. 2007. *The World Intellectual Property Organisation: Resurgence and the Development Agenda*. London, UK: Routledge.

May, Christopher and Susan Sell. 2006. *Intellectual Property Rights: A Critical History*. Boulder, CO: Lynne Rienner Publishers.

Merges, Robert P. 2000. Symposium on law in the twentieth century: one hundred years of solicitude: intellectual property law, 1900–2000. *California Law Review* 88(December): 2187–2240.

Mgbeoji, Ikechi. 2006. *Global Biopiracy: Patents, Plants and Indigenous Knowledge*. Vancouver, Canada: UBC Press.

Millaleo, Salvador and Hugo Cadenas. 2014. Intellectual property in Chile: problems and conflicts in a developing society. In David, Matthew and Debora J. Halbert (eds) *The Sage Handbook of Intellectual Property*. London, UK and Los Angeles, CA: Sage, 130–147.

Miller, Doug and Peter Williams. 2009. What price a living wage? Implementation issues in the quest for decent wages in the global apparel sector. *Global Social Policy* 9(1): 99–125.

Monsanto. 2014. Monsanto technology/stewardship agreement. Accessed 13 March 2015. http://www.siegers.com/pdfs/waivers/MonsantoTSA.pdf

Monsanto. 2015. Myth: Monsanto sells terminator seeds. http://www.monsanto. com/newsviews/pages/terminator-seeds.aspx Accessed 1 March 2015.

Moran, Warren. 1993. Rural space as intellectual property. *Political Geography* 12(3): 263–277.

Moran, Warren. 1999. The wine appellation as territory in France and California. *Annuls of the Association of American Geographers* 83(4): 694–717.

Morris, Sophie. 2011. Lounge life: take a seat ... and then copy it. *The Independent*, 25 November. http://www.independent.co.uk/property/interiors/lounge-life-take-a-seatand-then-copy-it-6267616.html

Mossoff, Adam. 2000. Rethinking the development of patents: an intellectual history, 1550–1800. *Hastings Law Journal* 52: 1255–1322.

Netanel, Neil. 2009. *The Development Agenda: Global Intellectual Property and Developing Countries*. Oxford, UK and New York, NY: Oxford University Press.

O'Brien, Dave. 2014. Creativity and copyright: the international career of a new economy. In David, Matthew and Debora J. Halbert (eds) *The Sage Handbook of Intellectual Property*. London, UK and Los Angeles, CA: Sage, 315–330.

Ochoa, Tyler T. 2010. Limits on the duration of copyright. In Parker, Jo Alyson, Paul A. Harris, and Christian Steinek (eds) *Time: Limits and Constraints*. Leiden, the Netherlands: Brill.

Ochoa, Tyler T. and Mark Rose. 2002. Anti-monopoly origins of the patent and copyright clause. *Journal of the Patent and Trademark Office Society* 84: 909–940.

Oguamanam, Chidi. 2006. *International Law and Indigenous Knowledge: Intellectual Property, Plant Biodiversity, and Traditional Medicine*. Toronto, Ontario: University of Toronto Press.

Oguamanam, Chidi. 2014. Farmers' rights and the intellectual property dynamic in agriculture. In David, Matthew and Debora J. Halbert (eds) *The Sage Handbook of Intellectual Property*. London, UK and Los Angeles, CA: Sage, 238–257.

Op den Kamp, Claudy. 2014. Copyright and film historiography: the case of the orphan film. In David, Matthew and Debora J. Halbert (eds) *The Sage Handbook of Intellectual Property*. London, UK and Los Angeles, CA: Sage, 404–417.

Pythian-Adams, Sarah Louisa. 2014. "The Economic Foundations of Intellectual Property: An Arts and Cultural Economist's Perspective." In David, Matthew and Debora J. Halbert (eds): 28–51.

Piketty, Thomas. 2014. *Capital in the Twenty-First Century*. Boston, MA: Harvard University Press.

Raustiala, Kal and Christopher Sprigman. 2012. *The Knockoff Economy: How Imitation Spurs Innovation*. Oxford, UK: Oxford University Press.

Rawls, John. 1971. *A Theory of Justice*. Boston, MA: Harvard University Press.

Richards, Donald. 2004. *Intellectual Property Rights and Global Capitalism: The Political Economy of the TRIPS Agreement*. Armonk, NY: M.E. Sharpe.

Rifkin, Jeremy. 2014. *The Zero Marginal Cost Society: The Internet of Things, the Collaborative Commons, and the Eclipse of Capitalism*. New York, NY: Palgrave.

Rimmer, Matthew. 2011. *Intellectual Property and Climate Change: Inventing Clean Technologies*. Cheltenham, UK and Northampton, MA: Edward Elgar.

Rimmer, Matthew. 2012. Patents for humanity. *The World Intellectual Property Organization WIPO Journal* 3(2): 196–221.

Rimmer, Matthew. 2014. Intellectual property and global warming: fossil fuels and climate justice. In David, Matthew and Debora J. Halbert (eds) *The Sage Handbook of Intellectual Property*. London, UK and Los Angeles, CA: Sage, 727–753.

Rojek, Chris. 2014. Counterfeit commerce: the illegal accumulation and distribution of intellectual property. In David, Matthew and Debora J. Halbert (eds) *The Sage Handbook of Intellectual Property*. London, UK and Los Angeles, CA: Sage, 189–206.

Rose, Mark. 1993. *Authors and Owners: The Invention of Copyright*. Cambridge, MA: Harvard University Press.

Ross, Andrew. 2009. *Nice Work If You Can Get It: Life and Labor in Precarious Times*. New York, NY: New York University Press.

Rousseau, Jean-Jacques. 2008. *The Social Contract*. Oxford, UK: Oxford World Classics.

Ryan, Michael P. 1998. *Knowledge Diplomacy: Global Competition and the Politics of Intellectual Property*. Washington, DC: Brookings Institution Press.

Sandell, Robert. 2007. Off the record. *Prospect Magazine*, 1 August. http://www.prospectmagazine.co.uk/features/offtherecord

Sandison, Hamish R. 1986. Berne Convention and the Universal Copyright Convention: the American experience. *Columbia-VLA Journal of Law & the Arts* 11: 89–120.

Schulte-Hillen, Catrin. 1999. Study concerning the availability and price of AZT. *Health Action International*, October. http://www.haiweb.org/campaign/novsem inar/schulte_text.html

Seidman, Lucy. 2007. *Beyond the Boycott: Labor Rights, Human Rights, and Transnational Activism*. New York, NY: Russell Sage Foundation.

Sell, Susan K. 2003. *Private Power, Public Law: The Globalization of Intellectual Property Rights*. Cambridge Studies in International Relations 88. Cambridge, UK: Cambridge University Press.

Sell, Susan K. 2004. Intellectual property and public policy in historical perspective: contestation and settlement. *Loyola of Los Angeles Law Review* 38(1): 267–322.

Sen, Amiti. 2012. India, Brazil & China defend generic drugs at WTO. *The Economic Times*, 25 June. http://articles.economictimes.indiatimes.com/2012-06-25/news/ 32409062_1_counterfeit-medicines-fake-drugs-generic-drugs

Sherman, Brad and Leanne Wiseman. 2006. Towards and indigenous public domain. In Lucie M. C. R. Guibault (ed.) *The Future of the Public Domain: Identifying the Commons in Information Law*. Alphen Aan Den Rijn, the Netherlands and Frederick, MD: Kluwer Law International and Aspen Publishers, 259–277.

Shiva, Vandana. 1997. *Biopiracy: The Plunder of Nature and Knowledge*. Boston, MA: South End Press.

Silbey, Jessica. 2014. *The Eureka Myth: Creators, Innovators, and Everyday Intellectual Property*. Stanford, CA: Stanford University Press.

Smiers, Joost and Marieke Van Schijndel. 2008. *Imagine–No Copyright*. Libertad y cambio; Variation: Colección Libertad y cambio. Barcelona, Spain: Barcelona Gedisa.

Smith, Linda Tuhiwai. 1999. *Decolonizing Methodologies: Research and Indigenous Peoples*. London, UK: Zed Books.

Spruill, W. Murray and Michelle Cunningham. 2005. Strategies for extending the life of patents. *International BioPharm*, March. http://www.alston.com/files/Pub lication/586807fa-b1be-4f2d-8915-6b383ac33233/Presentation/Publication Attachment/4a0e8595-d857-4772-8875-ac14b8fe109e/BioPharm%20Spruill %20May2005.pdf

Stolte, Keith M. 1998. How early did Anglo-American trademark law begin? An answer to Schechter's conundrum. *Fordham Intellectual Property, Media & Entertainment Law Journal* 8: 505–546.

Suthersanen, Uma. 2014. Copyright and industrial objects: aesthetic considerations and policy discriminations. In David, Matthew and Debora J. Halbert (eds) *The Sage Handbook of Intellectual Property*. London, UK and Los Angeles, CA: Sage, 539–562.

Tehranian, John. 2014. Dangerous undertakings: sacred texts and copyright's myth of aesthetic neutrality. In David, Matthew and Debora J. Halbert (eds) *The Sage Handbook of Intellectual Property*. London, UK and Los Angeles, CA: Sage, 418–429.

The National Bureau of Asian Research. 2013. *The IP Commission Report: The Report of the Commission on the Theft of American Intellectual Property*. Seattle, WA: The National Bureau of Asian Research. http://ipcommission.org/report/ IP_Commission_Report_052213.pdf

Thomas, Pradip. 2014. Copyright and copyleft in India: between global agendas and local interests. In David, Matthew and Debora J. Halbert (eds) *The Sage Handbook of Intellectual Property*. London, UK and Los Angeles, CA: Sage, 355–369.

Torremans, Paul. ed. 2008. *Intellectual Property and Human Rights: Enhanced Edition of Copyright and Human Rights*. Alphen Aan Den Rijn, the Netherlands and Frederick, MD: Kluwer Law and Aspen Publishers.

USPTO. 2014. Manual of Patent Evaluation Procedures, Chapter 2100, Section 2132. http://www.uspto.gov/web/offices/pac/mpep/s2132.html Accessed 28 November 2014.

Vaidhyanathan, Siva. 2003. *Copyrights and Copywrongs: The Rise of Intellectual Property and How It Threatens Creativity*. New York, NY: New York University Press.

Wall, Dave. 2014. Copyright trolling and the policing of intellectual property in the shadow of the law. In David, Matthew and Debora J. Halbert (eds) *The Sage Handbook of Intellectual Property*. London, UK and Los Angeles, CA: Sage, 607–626.

Wharton School. 2006. Generic drugs in Brazil are a hard pill for Big Pharma to swallow. *Knowledge@Wharton*, 1 March. http://knowledge.wharton.upenn.edu/article/generic-drugs-in-brazil-are-a-hard-pill-for-big-pharma-to-swallow

Whiteman, Natasha. 2014. Intellectual property and the construction of un/ethical audiences. In David, Matthew and Debora J. Halbert (eds) *The Sage Handbook of Intellectual Property*. London, UK and Los Angeles, CA: Sage, 470–489.

WIPO. 2014. WIPO-administered treaties. http://www.wipo.int/treaties/en/Show Results.jsp?lang=en&treaty_id=15 Accessed 3 May 2015.

WIPO. 2015a. Summary of the Paris Convention for the Protection of Industrial Property (1883). http://www.wipo.int/treaties/en/ip/paris/summary_paris.html Accessed 1 March 2015.

WIPO. 2015b. Patent Law Treaty (PLT) http://www.wipo.int/treaties/en/ip/plt Accessed 1 March 2015.

Wu, Tim. 2011. *The Master Switch: The Rise and Fall of Information Empires*. New York, NY: Vintage.

Yu, Peter K. 2004. *Currents and Crosscurrents in the International Intellectual Property Regime*. Occasional Papers in Intellectual Property & Communications Law, no. 5. East Lansing, MI: Michigan State University College of Law.

Yu, Peter K. 2014. Deja vu in the international intellectual property regime. In David, Matthew and Debora J. Halbert (eds) *The Sage Handbook of Intellectual Property*. London, UK and Los Angeles, CA: Sage, 113–129.

zotofoto. 2014. An indigenous feminist's take on the ontological turn: 'ontology' is just another word for colonialism. *Urbane Adventurer: Amiskwacî*, 24 October. http://zoeandthecity.wordpress.com/2014/10/24/an-indigenous-feminists-take-on-the-ontological-turn-ontology-is-just-another-word-for-colonialism

INDEX